Rock
COLLECTING
for Kids

An Introduction to Geology

Dan R. Lynch

Adventure Publications
Cambridge, Minnesota

DEDICATION AND ACKNOWLEDGMENTS

Thank you to my wife, Julie Kirsch, for her unending love, understanding, and support for my books and literally every other aspect of life.

And thank you to Emily Dix, Ron Pomper, and Steve Turnbull for their advice, encouragement, and enthusiasm for this project.

Edited by Brett Ortler
Cover and book design by Jonathan Norberg

Photo credits
Front cover: Jonathan Norberg (top)
All photos by Dan R. Lynch unless otherwise noted
NASA/NOAA GOES Project: 6, 33 (modified) **Shutterstock:** front cover (bottom), 7 (bottom), 12, 13, 15, 16 (both), 18, 20, 21, 22 (both), 23, 28 (bottom), 31 (top), 33 (top), 36 (quartz), 38, 40 (fingernail, nickel, apatite, knife), 41 (ceramic tile, steel file, corundum, drill bit, diamond ring), 45 (all), 46 (both), 47, 53 (coral, sand, mud), 81 (corundum, diamond), 117 (amber), 120 (top), 123, 124, 125, 128, 129, 132 (both), 133

15 14 13 12 11 10 9

Rock Collecting for Kids

Rock
COLLECTING
for **Kids**

TABLE OF CONTENTS

All About Geology

If you want to collect rocks, it helps to know a little about geology. **Geology** is the study of the Earth and what it's made of. Geology also explores the Earth's history and how it has changed since it formed long ago.

A scientist who works in geology is called a **geologist**. A geologist studies **rocks** and **minerals** and everything else about the Earth beneath our feet.

Rocks and minerals
are very important
to understand
because they make up
the Earth and because we
use them every day. We use rocks
to build houses and walls, and we use minerals
to make many things, like coins, computers, and glass.
But we can also use rocks and minerals
to learn amazing things, like the
age of the Earth and what
kinds of animals lived long ago.

Rocks and minerals are also
fun to collect! By picking
up rocks and writing down
where you found them, you can
learn a lot about geology. And
you can build your collection
every time you visit a new place.
But you're not
allowed to collect
just anywhere!
Check out page 126
to make sure it's OK to
collect where you are. And
when in doubt, ask first!

OUR EARTH

The Earth is always changing. The mountains, oceans, and rocks seem like they will be here forever. But they will be gone someday, and something new will be in their place. These changes happen because of the Earth's geology.

The Earth is made up of layers. The outside of the Earth, where all the plants, animals, and people live, is called the **crust**. The crust is like a thin, hard shell of rock on the surface of the planet. It has all the mountains, plains, oceans, and deserts that we see, but the crust is affected by the layers beneath it.

Deeper inside the Earth, there is another layer called the **mantle**. It is very hot and made up of melted rock. It's so far down that we can't dig there. The melted rock in the mantle is called magma. The mantle's heat is like a big oven, and all of that heat causes the crust above it to move around. Sometimes the magma pushes its way up through the crust—we call that a volcano!

Deeper down, there are even hotter layers, and some of those layers are melted and others are solid. At the very center of the Earth is a hot, solid **core** made of metal.

When we study geology, we look at what the Earth is made of and how the inside of the Earth moves and changes. Geology also involves how the weather can change the Earth's surface long-term. Over a long time, wind, rain, and ice can wear down rocks, and even whole mountains can be worn away!

INSIDE THE EARTH

THE CRUST
The ground, mountains, and the ocean are all part of the thin outer crust.

UPPER MANTLE
Located just underneath the crust, the upper mantle is hot and soft because it is made up of melted rock.

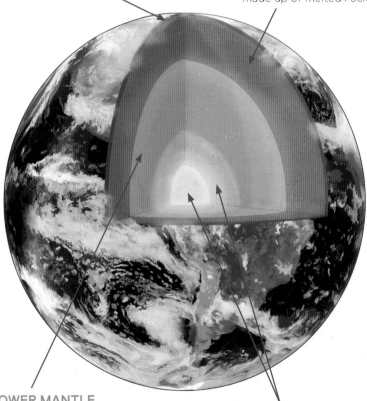

LOWER MANTLE
The lower mantle is made of rocks that won't melt because they're buried too deep, even though it is very hot.

OUTER AND INNER CORE
The outer core is so hot that everything there melts and swirls around the inner core, which is made up of solid metal!

LANDFORMS AND TECTONIC PLATES

Hills, mountains, and canyons are all examples of **landforms**, or features that occur on Earth. But have you ever looked at a mountain or an ocean and wondered how it formed? In most cases, it's because of tectonic plates.

The thin outer crust of the Earth is made of many separate pieces, which are called **tectonic plates**. These plates fit together like giant puzzle pieces. Tectonic plates are always moving because of the hot, melted rock flowing underneath them. Some plates move away from each other, some crash into each other, and some slide past each other. These different actions can make all kinds of landforms, such as mountains, valleys, and even volcanoes! Most of the continents sit on top of their own tectonic plate, while most oceans are on top of more than one. The map below shows all of the Earth's most important plates, which are outlined in yellow.

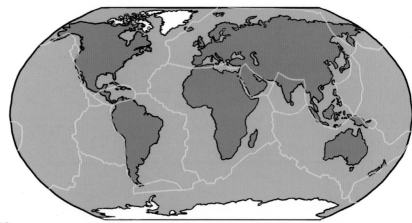

Let's look at a few ways tectonic plates can move:

CONVERGENT MOVEMENT
(coming together)

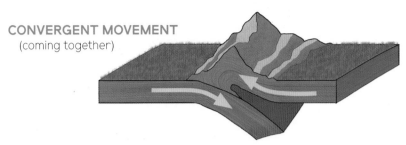

When two plates smash into each other, sometimes one is forced under (where the rock melts) and the other is pushed upward. This can make mountains.

DIVERGENT MOVEMENT
(separating)

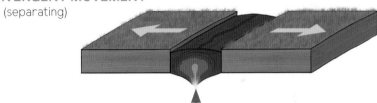

At the bottom of the ocean, plates are often pushed apart by rising magma (melted rock). This creates underwater mountain ranges; plates moving apart on land produce valleys that eventually become seas.

TRANSFORM MOVEMENT
(sliding past)

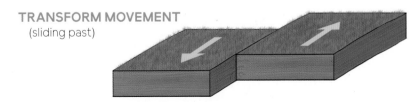

Sometimes two plates just slide past each other. As they grind along, this can cause powerful earthquakes that shake the land. Earthquakes happen every day, but most are too small to feel.

The Grand Canyon is an amazing example of how water alone can cut an enormous path through rock.

WEATHERING

Most rocks seem very hard and solid. But have you ever found a rock that crumbled very easily? Or have you seen a giant rock formation with a hole in it? Those things happened because of weathering. **Weathering** happens when rain, wind, waves, and ice wear down rocks over a long time. Even the round pebbles you find at the beach are weathered—when the strong waves pushed them around, the pebbles tumbled into each other and were worn smooth.

Sometimes weathering can happen to very large rocks or rock formations. Rivers weather rocks when the movement of water carries away sediment (pieces of the rock). Over time, so much sediment can be carried away that the river gets deeper. Arizona's Grand Canyon was created when a river carved through the rocks for many years.

Wind can weather rocks too. In deserts, the wind can blow sand around very easily. When the little, hard grains of sand hit other rocks, they begin to break them into pieces. The softer areas of rock break down first. Sometimes when the soft areas are surrounded by harder areas, the softer rock can wear away to form a hole or an arch.

Even plants can weather rocks! When trees and other plants get their roots into cracks, they can split the rocks apart as the roots grow bigger. On the sides of mountains or on the edges of cliffs, this can make rocks fall apart and tumble down. When you see a pile of rock at the bottom of a mountain, you know that plants, along with water and ice, got into cracks and broke the rock into pieces.

These rock arches in Wyoming are famous examples of weathering caused by wind.

EXAMPLES OF WEATHERING

ARCHES
These are amazing examples of how wind and blowing sand can weather rocks.

PILLARS AND MESAS
Rock pillars and flat-topped mesas are formed by erosion caused by wind and rain.

wind

CLIFF
Cliffs form when water and plants weather rocks and cause them to fall.

SCREE
Scree is the rubble and rock that falls off a mountain or cliff. It often falls into a pile.

RIVER VALLEYS AND CANYONS
These V-shaped canyons are made by rivers that cut down into the rock over time.

Stalactites are amazing hanging rocks that are found in caves. The ones above are from Carlsbad Caverns National Park in New Mexico.

CAVES

A **cave** is an opening in rock, usually underground. You've probably seen pictures of a dark cave before, but did you know that many caves are formed by weathering?

There is a lot of water underground. It is called **groundwater**. When we dig a well to find drinking water, groundwater is what comes out. But some rocks, especially limestone, can dissolve in groundwater, just like sugar dissolves in water. In time, groundwater can dissolve and wash away rocks, creating openings. Those openings are called caves.

A sinkhole in a desert in Israel.

Sometimes a big cave can weaken the ground above it. If the ground above a cave can't hold itself up anymore, it falls in. This is called a **sinkhole**, and large sinkholes can even make buildings or cars fall into the ground. Thankfully, dangerous sinkholes are very rare. Sinkholes are more common in tropical areas, and in Mexico

The dark insides of a cenote in Mexico.

there are some very big sinkholes called **cenote** (say it, "sih-no-tee"). They are popular places to visit because they have water at the bottom.

SINKHOLES, CENOTES, AND MORE

SINKHOLES
Sinkholes form when groundwater weakens and washes away underground rock.

CENOTE
This large sinkhole has groundwater at the bottom; it is called a cenote.

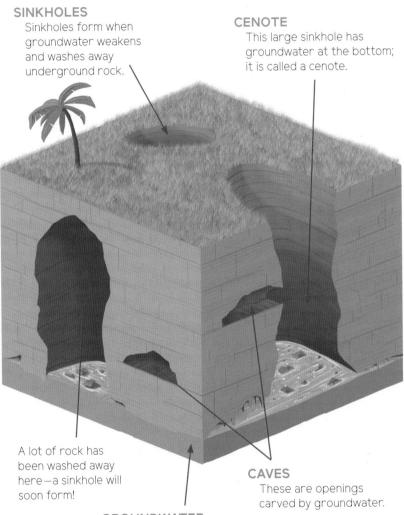

A lot of rock has been washed away here—a sinkhole will soon form!

CAVES
These are openings carved by groundwater.

GROUNDWATER
Water that flows through rocks, often deep underground.

GLACIERS

Weathering and erosion from wind and rain can make landforms like canyons and cliffs. But some of the biggest changes to the land happened because of glaciers. During the last **ice age**, when the world was colder, glaciers covered a lot of the northern parts of the world. And when the glaciers disappeared, they left behind lakes, valleys, and rivers. But what is a glacier?

Glaciers are huge masses of ice that form when tons of snow builds up and turns into ice over a long period of time. As a glacier continues to form, it spreads out across the land, moving and flowing almost like a very slow river. Many of the glaciers in the last ice age were thousands of feet thick and many miles wide!

This glacier in Switzerland shows the dirty ice flowing downhill and melting into a lake. Do you see the valley that the glacier has carved?

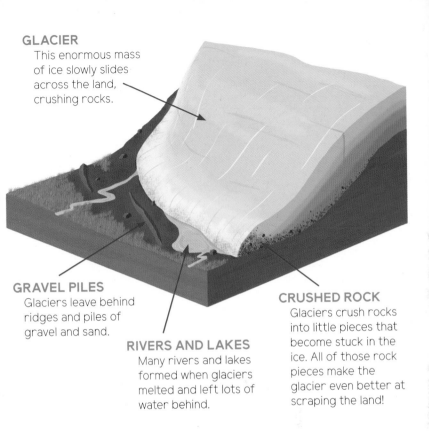

GLACIER
This enormous mass of ice slowly slides across the land, crushing rocks.

GRAVEL PILES
Glaciers leave behind ridges and piles of gravel and sand.

RIVERS AND LAKES
Many rivers and lakes formed when glaciers melted and left lots of water behind.

CRUSHED ROCK
Glaciers crush rocks into little pieces that become stuck in the ice. All of those rock pieces make the glacier even better at scraping the land!

Glaciers only move a few feet each day, but they weigh so much that they crush the rocks that they move over. Glaciers can even grind down hills, carve valleys into rock, and flatten the entire landscape!

During the ice age, the glaciers formed in cold northern parts of the world and slowly moved south. As the ice of a glacier moved, it picked up lots of broken rock and gravel.

All of these smooth, shiny rocks were worn flat by a glacier that once moved through this valley. Do you see the lines on the rock made by the scraping ice?

But when the glaciers melted, the rock was left behind in piles, which we can see today as hills. All of that melting ice also created lots of rivers, lakes, and other landforms. In some places in the world, you can still find big, smooth rocks with lots of deep scratches in them, which show how the glaciers scraped them as they passed through the area.

ROCK FORMATIONS

All the landforms you see every day, like mountains and lakes, were formed by the Earth's geology. These changes are caused mostly by the moving tectonic plates and by weathering. But some of these landforms often developed in different ways. Knowing how they formed can help you know whether they are good places to look for rocks and minerals.

Mountains and some hills form when rocks are forced upward by tectonic plate movement. Lots of rocks from deep in the Earth can be pushed up to where we can find them. Sometimes you can find gemstones, crystals, and even fossils in the rocks of mountains.

The Matterhorn Mountain in Switzerland is an awesome example of a mountain formed when tectonic plate movement forced rocks upward.

Rivers and lakes usually form due to weathering. Here's how it works: Wind and rain make a low spot in the Earth where water collects. As more water collects there, it forms rivers and lakes, where water begins to flow and move. This can move lots of rocks and even wear them away. When a river carves into rocks over many years, it can form a canyon. On the shores of lakes and rivers, you can often find neat rocks and minerals that have been worn smooth and round by water.

Oceans form when tectonic plates spread apart and leave a gap between them. As the gap gets bigger and bigger, it fills with water. Oceans are so powerful that they can move and weather lots of rocks. On the shores of oceans and seas, you can find many kinds of rocks and minerals, as well as seashells and even fossils.

Deserts are regions that don't get much rain, and they are very dry. Deserts usually form because

This giant gold mine in Australia is an example of mining today. Lots of mining is done by digging enormous pits like this.

they are in a hot part of the world, and often there are mountains that block them from getting rain. There aren't a lot of plants in deserts, so rocks are usually easy to see on the ground. This can make it easy to find neat rocks and minerals.

Mines are places where people dig lots of minerals out of the ground. When people dig into the ground to find valuable metals or gemstones, it's called mining. Sometimes mines are tunnels that go deep underground, and other times mines are giant open pits in the ground. Mines can be found in mountains, hills, deserts, and anywhere in between.

Minerals

Rocks and minerals are two very different things. Rocks are made up of mixtures of lots of different minerals. But minerals are more pure; they are chemicals that have hardened. This means that minerals are always made of the same stuff, but rocks can be a mixture of lots of different things. This makes minerals special because we can use them to figure out what our world is made of. And once you understand minerals and the rocks they formed in, you're one step closer to figuring out where to find crystals and gems to collect!

WHAT MAKES A MINERAL?

Minerals form when specific chemicals join together and harden. For example, table salt is a mineral. It is a combination of two chemical elements: sodium and chlorine. Elements are basically "building blocks," and each mineral has its own recipe of chemical elements. (This is called the mineral's chemical formula.) There are thousands of minerals in the world. They can be found as grains in all kinds of rocks, but they also can be found on their own.

HOW MINERALS FORM

Minerals form in many ways. A lot of minerals form when very hot water comes up from the Earth and gets into holes or cracks in rocks and dries up. That hot water often has tiny particles of minerals in it, and when it dries up and cools off, it leaves minerals behind.

You can also test this at home! Put a little salt in some warm water, and stir it up until the salt disappears (dissolves). Then let the water dry up. When it's dry, you'll see a crust of tiny salt crystals left over.

Other minerals form when rocks weather. When rocks are exposed to water, they break down and their ingredients separate, freeing the minerals inside it.

CRYSTALS

If a mineral has enough room when it is forming, it can form a crystal. **Crystals** are hard shapes that are made of a pure mineral. Each mineral has its own crystal shape (or shapes). Some crystals can be pointy, and others can be flat or square. They can also be different colors, some can be see-through, and some are shiny.

Mineral collectors love crystals, which can be hard to find. Most are found inside holes or spaces in rocks. Collectors often break rocks to find them. Some minerals can be found loose in the dirt or on a beach, but most must be dug up out of the ground.

This is a piece of a mineral called marcasite. It's actually a group of marcasite crystals. Look at all the amazing details on the crystals, like the little ridges and different colors!

HOW CRYSTAL FORMATION HAPPENS

A simplified look at one of the many ways minerals form.

NO MINERALS
No groundwater with minerals in it has reached this empty space, so no minerals are forming here.

EMPTY SPACES IN ROCK
Many minerals form in the empty spaces in rock, such as these holes, which were made by trapped gases in cooling lava (molten rock).

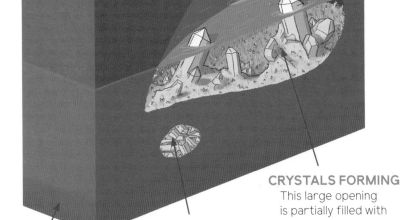

HOT WATER
Heat from deep in the Earth warms up water and adds lots of minerals to it.

FILLED WITH CRYSTALS
This hole was small and is totally filled by mineral crystals.

CRYSTALS FORMING
This large opening is partially filled with warm, mineral-rich groundwater, so big and small crystals are forming inside.

WHAT DO MINERALS LOOK LIKE?

There are thousands of minerals in the world, but minerals are usually only found in three ways: as parts of a rock, as individual crystals, or as loose pebbles.

When you see a speckled rock with lots of different colors, look at it closely. You can see that each colored chunk is a separate grain. Those grains are minerals!

You can also find minerals as crystals. These hard shapes can often be found inside holes in rocks. Next time you find a rock with a hole in it, look inside. If you see little sparkly shapes, those are mineral crystals!

Minerals can also be found as loose pebbles. Have you ever been on a beach or at a river and found a white pebble that lets light shine through it? Or maybe you have found a black pebble that looks shiny, like metal? Those are minerals that water helped free from rock.

THE MANY FORMS A MINERAL CAN TAKE

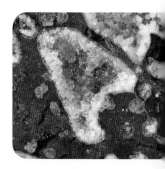

Quartz is a very common mineral, and it forms in many ways and in many places. It also can look pretty different, depending on how you find it. When it is very well-formed, it looks like big, pointy crystals that are white and see-through.

When quartz forms in tiny openings in rock, it can look like many little, pointy, sparkly crystals all over the inside of the hole.

One of the most common ways to find quartz is as a part of rocks. This speckly, grainy rock is a kind of granite, and most of the white you see is quartz.

Another common way to find quartz is on beaches or rivers as white pebbles. Long ago, these might have been crystals, but because of weathering, this quartz has been rounded and worn down into smooth stone.

CRYSTAL SHAPES

The best way to learn about minerals is to look at their crystals. Many minerals only have one crystal shape, but others can have many different shapes depending on where they formed! Here are just a few examples.

This is calcite, and it can form as sharp, pointy crystals. But it can also form as clusters of block-shaped crystals. Or it can form in cracks in rocks. These are just three ways that calcite can form. It can have hundreds of different crystal shapes!

Pointy
Some minerals
form big, pointy
crystals, like
quartz does.

Round
Some crystals, such as
garnet, are shaped
almost like soccer balls.

Cube
Minerals like pyrite can
form as cubes and look
just like blocks!

Flaky
Some minerals,
like mica, form
as big groups of
flaky, thin crystals.

Blocky
Feldspar often forms as crude, rectangle-shaped blocks in rocks.

Lumpy
Some minerals, like turquoise, show no crystal shape and instead are just lumpy masses.

Grape-like
Hematite is an example of a mineral that forms in lumpy chunks that look like bunches of grapes!

Tree-like
This crystal of copper is very complex. It is made up of many smaller shapes that make it look like a tree!

MINERAL COLORS

Minerals occur in many colors, and some minerals are found in more than one color. Quartz is one example, and its color variations even have special names.

Quartz is normally very clear or white.

Sometimes it can be gray or black and is known as smoky quartz.

It can also sometimes be pink, which we call rose quartz.

Purple quartz is called amethyst.

STREAK COLOR

Some minerals can seem to change color when they are crushed into a powder. This is important to know because some minerals can be identified by the color of their powder. For example, hematite is a shiny black mineral, but when it is crushed, it looks rusty red.

But you don't have to crush a whole specimen to see what color its powder is. You can also scratch it on a special piece of tile called a "streak plate." When you scratch a mineral on this plate, it leaves behind a powdered **streak** of color.

Not all minerals will leave a streak. Usually only softer minerals leave a streak behind. (The harder minerals will just scratch the plate!) But it can still be useful to figure out what mineral you have found.

If you want a streak plate of your own, have an adult help you find a piece of unglazed porcelain—it works just the same as a special streak plate!

Hematite is a metallic black mineral, but it has a red-brown streak.

Goethite is a metallic black-brown mineral, but it has a yellow-brown streak.

Pyrite is a metallic brass-colored mineral, but it has a dark green-black streak.

LUSTER

Aside from shape, color, and streak, minerals also have luster. **Luster** is how shiny a mineral is. Some minerals are shiny like glass or metal. Others are not shiny at all.

We compare the luster of a mineral to the luster of another material. For example, if a mineral is shiny like glass, we say it has glassy luster. Or if it is shiny and reflective, like a metal, it has a metallic luster.

Here are some examples:

Quartz is glassy.

Jasper can be waxy.

Limonite is earthy.

Feldspars can be dull.

Serpentine is greasy.

Gold is always metallic.

Opal

Some minerals have an even more dramatic appearance. Opal is normally glassy, but some special opals have areas that seem to glow with a rainbow of colors. These colors change and flash as you turn the stone. This is called

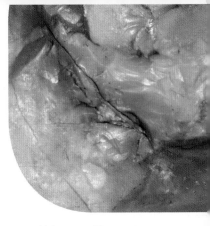

opalescence. You can sometimes see this on other materials, too, such as the inside of some seashells.

Labradorite

A mineral called labradorite is also a lot of fun to look at. It has lots of tiny layers inside of it, and when light hits those layers, it can make bright flashes of color. As you move the stone, those colors can change or disappear. You have to hold it at just the right angle to see them. This is called **labradorescence**.

Labradorite at the wrong angle.   Labradorite at the right angle.

HARDNESS

There's one other thing to test to help you identify a mineral: its hardness. Hardness tells you how easy it is to scratch a mineral. Some minerals are so soft that you can scratch them with your fingernails. Other minerals are so hard that they can scratch glass. All minerals have a definite hardness. If you know how to check the hardness of a mineral, identifying it can be much easier.

Mineral hardness is measured on a scale of 1 to 10. A mineral with a hardness of 1 is very soft, and 10 is very hard. Most minerals are in the middle, between 3 and 7. So how do you check a mineral's hardness? To test hardness you try to scratch a mineral with something you already know the hardness of. For a chart with the hardness of common materials and everyday objects (known as the Mohs hardness scale), see page 40. When you're testing minerals, make sure you have an adult's help. Some of the tools are sharp, so be careful. Also, don't press too hard. It shouldn't take a lot of pressure to see if the tool will scratch the mineral.

For example, your fingernail has a hardness of 2. So if your fingernail scratches your mineral, you know that your mineral is softer than a 2.5 on the scale. Or, if a U.S. nickel coin (a 3.5 on the scale) scratches your mineral, you know that your mineral is softer than a 3.5. Some minerals have some variation, so they can be a little softer or harder in places.

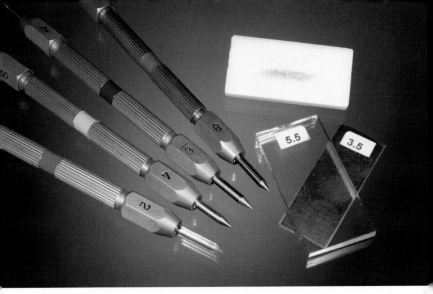

A kit used to test minerals for hardness.

IDENTIFYING YOUR FIND (WITH AN ADULT'S HELP)

After you test with one tool, try another and narrow down the mineral's hardness. For example, if a knife scratches your mineral, you know it is softer than a 5.5, but that doesn't help much. If you then use a U.S. nickel and it still scratches the mineral, now you know it is softer than 3.5. But if your fingernail does not scratch it, you know it is harder than 2.5. This would make the mineral a 3 in hardness. This is how you can narrow down the hardness. Then you can use the mineral's hardness and appearance to find similar minerals. To get started, turn to page 40 in this book!

Example Mineral

MOHS HARDNESS SCALE

Tool

TALC — 1

GYPSUM — 2

FINGERNAIL

2.5

CALCITE — 3

3.5

U.S. NICKEL

FLUORITE — 4

GLASS, or
a STEEL
KNIFE

APATITE — 5

5.5

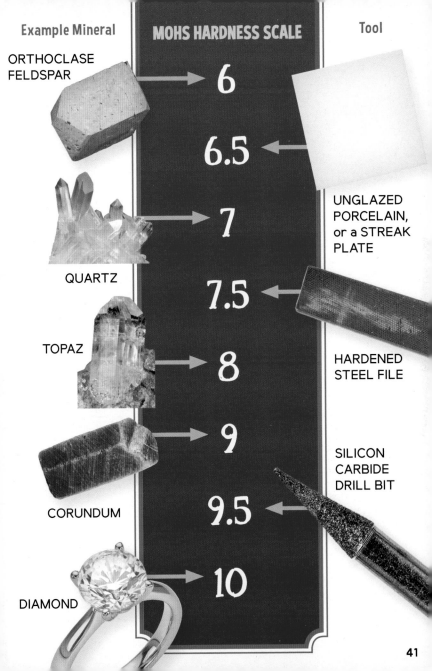

Example Mineral

MOHS HARDNESS SCALE

Tool

ORTHOCLASE
FELDSPAR

6

6.5

UNGLAZED
PORCELAIN,
or a STREAK
PLATE

7

QUARTZ

7.5

TOPAZ

8

HARDENED
STEEL FILE

9

SILICON
CARBIDE
DRILL BIT

CORUNDUM

9.5

10

DIAMOND

41

Rocks

Rocks make up the Earth's surface, and they are such familiar objects in everyday life that we take them for granted. But rocks tell you a lot about the area they are found in, including whether collectible minerals or fossils might be nearby. In this section, we'll learn about the three main kinds of rocks, how they form, and why they're important to know.

ALL ABOUT ROCKS

Rocks give the land its shapes and features, like high mountains and the ground beneath our feet. There are many different kinds of rocks, but all rocks share something in common: **All rocks are made of minerals, and each kind of rock has a different mixture of minerals in it**.

The kinds of minerals found in a rock determine what color it is, how hard it is, and where it is found. Some rocks are full of layers, some are speckly, and some are just a solid color.

Because rocks are made of many different minerals, they can't be tested for hardness or streak like minerals can, but a rock's appearance can still tell you a lot about it.

For example, this rock is called gneiss (say it, "nice"), and you can see it has many layers and different colored spots. Those are valuable clues to help you identify it, but only if you know about the three main kinds of rocks first.

WHAT'S IN A ROCK?

Rocks are made up of a mixture of different minerals. Each kind of rock has a different mix of minerals. This piece of granite contains mica, feldspar, quartz, pyroxene, and many other minerals! If that mixture were different, it'd be a different kind of rock.

Quartz

Pyroxene

Feldspar

Mica

ROCKS: WHAT'S ON THE GROUND AND HOW DID IT GET THERE?

Rocks are everywhere—from the ground underneath our feet to the peaks of the Rockies and the Appalachians. But how are rocks formed in the first place?

igneous

There are three main ways that rocks form. Some rocks form when hot, melted rock cools off—these are called **igneous rocks** (say it, "ig-nee-us"). Some igneous rocks cool off very slowly deep in the Earth. Others cool off quickly when lava is exposed on the surface.

sedimentary

Sedimentary rocks (say it, "sed-i-ment-air-ee") form when many little grains of material, such as sand, stick together over long periods of time. This creates "beds" of material that eventually harden into rock.

metamorphic

And sometimes, old rocks are heated up so much or are pressed together so hard that they become different rocks. These are called **metamorphic rocks** (say it, "met-a-morf-ik").

IGNEOUS ROCKS

Even though the ground beneath your feet is very hard, it is much softer deep below. That's because it is very hot underground—so hot that it can even melt rocks! It's weird to think about it, but there are oceans of melted rock under the ground. The soft, melted rock underground is called **magma**.

Just like water, magma moves and flows around. It is always moving, but very slowly, and all the hard rocks on Earth float on top of the magma. This means that everything on Earth's surface moves, and this includes

everything from mountains to continents. Sometimes (see page 10), tectonic plates can even bump into one another.

When a crack forms in the Earth, magma from deep underground can rise and flow out where we can see it. This is called a **volcano**.

And when magma flows from a volcano out onto the Earth's surface, the magma is called **lava**. When lava comes out of a volcano, a lot of gas and crushed rock (called ash) comes out with it. This is called an **eruption**. As soon as lava has erupted from a volcano, it begins to cool and harden. And when it hardens, it becomes rock.

But magma deep in the Earth can cool and harden to become rock, too. It just takes a lot longer for it to cool when it is still underground. And when magma cools slowly, the minerals inside it have a lot of time to become crystals. This makes the rock very chunky and coarse, with lots of speckled colors. Granite is a famous example of one rock that took a long time to cool.

Mount Etna, a volcano in Italy, erupting from the Voragine crater.

HOW VOLCANOES WORK

GAS AND ASH
When a volcano erupts, lots of gas and crushed rock, called ash, gets thrown into the sky.

VOLCANO
A volcano is a vent in the Earth's crust where magma can rise up out of the ground.

LAVA
Molten rock that has been forced outside a volcano is called lava, and it flows slowly away from the volcano.

COOLING ROCK
Outside a volcano, lava cools to form new rocks.

MAGMA
Below a volcano is a big mass of magma, which is molten rock deep underground. When magma is forced upwards, it can form a volcano.

COOLING DOWN

When lava cools, the minerals in it begin to harden and crystallize. Some minerals crystallize before others, and the longer they take, the bigger they can grow. When lava is still very hot, there are very few crystals in it. But as it cools, there are more and more crystals and they get bigger and bigger until the rock is cool. All of those crystals have to share the same space, so they fit together tightly like puzzle pieces. So you can think of igneous rocks as jigsaw puzzles full of minerals!

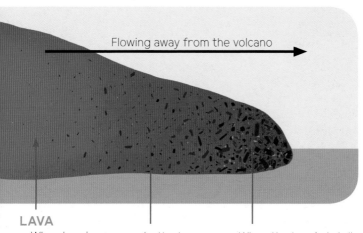

Flowing away from the volcano

LAVA

When lava is very hot, few crystals have formed.

As the lava begins to cool, small crystals start to form.

When the lava is totally cool, lots of different mineral crystals have formed and are stuck together to form rock.

But things are different when lava cools on the Earth's surface. When magma cools deep in the Earth, crystals have more time to form, making different rocks.

When lava hardens into rock, it can look different depending on how deep in the Earth it cooled. All of the rocks shown on this page contain the same mineral mixture or "recipe." They just cooled at different depths.

Pumice forms at the very top of a lava flow. When lava erupts to the surface, it has lots of gas in it. The gas tries to rise out of the lava, just like the bubbles in fizzy soda. But the lava can harden with all of those bubbles still inside it. Pumice has so many bubbles that some pieces can float on water!

Rhyolite forms when this type of lava erupts onto the Earth's surface. When it gets out into the cool air, it cools very quickly. This means that it has very small mineral grains. Rhyolite can also have lines that show how the lava flowed before it hardened.

Granite is a very common rock that forms when a certain kind of magma cools deep within the Earth. It cooled slowly, which gave the minerals inside it time to form large grains. The large mineral grains give it a spotted, colorful look.

Pegmatite forms deep in the magma. It looks a lot like granite, but with much larger crystals in it—and sometimes valuable gems! It can form when deep magma cools very slowly or when magma contains lots of water, which helps its crystals grow.

This is just one example. There are lots of families of rocks that all contain the same ingredients but formed at different places in the Earth.

SEDIMENTARY ROCKS

When old rocks are exposed to water and wind for too long, they start to crack and wear away. When rocks break down for a long time, they turn into sand or mud, just like at the bottom of a river or a pond. Sand, mud, and other grains of rocks or plant and animal material are called sediments. After a while, sediments can stick together and become a new rock. This is how many sedimentary rocks are formed.

Sometimes, dead plants and animals can fall into wet sediment. When the plant or animal is buried quickly, it becomes trapped inside the sediment. Then, when the sediment sticks together and becomes a sedimentary rock, the plants and animals inside turn into

fossil coral

rock, too. When this happens, it is called a **fossil**. Fossils are the preserved parts of ancient plants and animals.

Fossils of dinosaurs are very exciting and well known, but they are also very rare. Other fossils are much more common. Things like snail shells, leaves, and coral are very common as fossils. Many times, the fossils we find are of animals that are extinct, which means they no longer live anywhere on Earth. We can learn a lot about ancient life by studying fossils.

Some special kinds of sedimentary rocks are made up entirely of animal remains, such as coral. Coral is a type of tiny animal that lives in the ocean in large groups. Each coral makes a hard outer shell. After a long time, the hard shells build up into a large mass called a colony. When many hard colonies grow in one place, it is called a coral reef. Long ago, ancient coral reefs got so big that they turned into giant masses of rock called limestone. Limestone is completely made up of fossils!

Sedimentary Rock Formation

SAND AND MUD
Loose sand and mud begin to build up in thick layers.

SEDIMENTS
Sediments, like sand or the remains of coral, settle to the bottom of a lake or ocean.

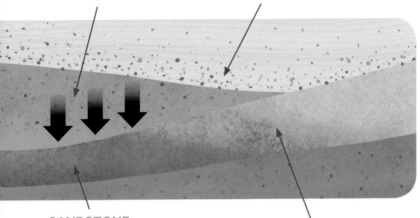

SANDSTONE
When sediments like sand are buried and pressed by lots of weight, they can harden to form rocks like sandstone.

Sediments that are not buried may not harden together and will just remain as loose sand and mud.

Some Examples of How Sedimentary Rocks Form

Coral reefs in ancient seas

. . . became limestone.

Sand in ancient lakes

. . . became sandstone.

Mud in ancient seas

. . . became shale.

METAMORPHIC ROCKS

The last way rocks can form is when old rocks are turned into new rocks through a process called **metamorphism**. This can happen in a few different ways. One way it can happen is when old rocks are buried and heated up underground. When the rocks get heated up, they get a little soft and start to change. They often become layered and grow large crystals. Old rocks can also be changed when hot magma underground touches them.

Another way that old rocks can change is when they become buried by tons of rocks above them. This presses them very hard, and they become layered. The layers in these rocks can be very thin and are stuck together very tightly.

Sometimes both heat and pressure can change an old rock into a new kind of rock.

Metamorphic rocks are especially interesting for collectors because they can hold gems inside, too! For example, look at this garnet gem, which formed in a metamorphic rock called skarn.

How Metamorphic Rocks Form

As this layer of rock gets buried deeper and deeper, the weight from above and heat from below change it more and more.

UPPER ROCK LAYERS
Rocks higher up in the Earth press down on the rocks deeper below.

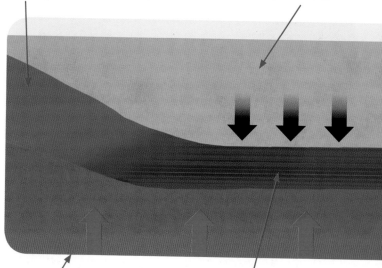

HEAT
Heat from deep in the Earth can rise and soften the rocks above it.

CHANGING ROCK
This rock layer is being pressed from above and heated from below, so it is compacting, forming layers, and becoming a new kind of rock.

Some Examples of How Metamorphic Rocks Form

Limestone, under heat and pressure . . .

. . . becomes marble.

Basalt, under heat and pressure . . .

. . . becomes greenstone.

Shale, under pressure . . .

. . . becomes slate.

Once you understand what kinds of rocks there are and where to find them, you can start to learn the different minerals that come along with them! These cool red crystals are a mineral called vanadinite, and you can see that they are growing right off the surface of this metamorphic rock from Arizona.

How to Identify Rocks and Minerals

Now that you know the differences between rocks and minerals, it's time to start identifying them! But how do you figure out what kind of rock or mineral you found? There are many kinds of both rocks and minerals, so it all comes down to observation. Once you've noted the color, shape, hardness and luster of a piece that you have found, this section will help you learn how to use that information to identify your find. You'll also read about some of the most common and important rocks and minerals that you could find. Read these pages carefully, then grab a magnifying glass and start identifying your collection!

DO I HAVE A ROCK OR A MINERAL?

When you have found a neat specimen and want to identify it, one of the first steps is to figure out if it is a rock or a mineral. Often, this is easy—but not always. Sometimes a mineral can appear very much like a rock. Before you try to identify your discoveries, here are some questions to answer to see if you have a rock or a mineral.

GRANITE Notice all the different colored mineral grains.

CAN YOU SEE GRAINS, ESPECIALLY DIFFERENT COLORED GRAINS?

Many rocks, such as granite, are obviously rocks because you can see all of the different colored minerals within them. This can be difficult to see on fine-grained rocks, like basalt, but if you use a magnifying glass, you will still find lots of tiny, different grains. Many rocks with visible grains are igneous, like those starting on page 68.

BASALT The mineral grains are tiny, but they are still there!

Minerals do not show different colored grains and instead look like they are made of only one material.

FELDSPAR This piece may look like a rock, but it has no grains!

CAN YOU SEE AIR BUBBLES?

Rocks like basalt and rhyolite often have empty bubbles in them made by gasses when the rocks were still soft. Minerals almost never have bubbles in them. Rocks with air bubbles are igneous rocks (page 46).

BUBBLES This basalt pebble has lots of air bubbles (called vesicles).

IS THERE A LOT OF IT AROUND?

When you find a neat rock, there are often many, many pieces of it around. Minerals are usually a little more rare, and you may have to search a little longer to find another piece. So if you find something neat and there is a lot of it on the ground, it's probably a rock.

IS IT GRITTY TO THE TOUCH? DOES IT CRUMBLE EASILY?

If something you find is very gritty and rough with lots of little sharp grains, it is probably a rock. Similarly, if you find something that is crumbling and dirty when you pick it up, it is also probably a rock. Many times, gritty and crumbly rocks are sedimentary rocks; check out page 70 for examples.

SHALE This loose, crumbly chunk is a rock.

DOES IT HAVE LOTS OF LAYERS?

Many rocks have layers or stripes of color in them. Sometimes they are flat and thin; sometimes they can be wide and wavy. And other times, these layers can split apart and separate. If you find a specimen with lots of layers, it could be a metamorphic rock (page 72) or a sedimentary (page 70) one.

SHALE These thin, layered sheets form a rock called shale.

IS IT GLASSY OR SEE-THROUGH?

GYPSUM Some gypsum can be see-through and shiny like glass.

PREHNITE This rounded pebble can have waxy surfaces.

If you find something that is a little shiny, kind of like glass, then it is probably a mineral because very few rocks are very glassy. And if you find something that lets light shine through it or that you can see through, it is probably a mineral. Try looking through the glassy minerals starting on page 80 or the waxy minerals starting on page 91.

IS IT SHINY LIKE METAL?

When you find something that is very shiny and looks like metal, it could be a mineral. Most rocks are not metallic, but many minerals are. Sometimes you may find a shiny metallic mineral spot inside a rock, too. Check out the metallic minerals starting on page 95.

COPPER One of the most well-known metallic minerals.

MAGNETITE This mineral is nearly always black and metallic.

CALCITE When calcite breaks, it makes lots of little edges, like stair steps.

DOES IT HAVE LOTS OF LITTLE EDGES THAT ALL GO IN THE SAME DIRECTION?

Many minerals break apart at certain angles. Some minerals, like calcite, can show lots of edges with the same angle and direction. Rocks don't really do this, so if you have a piece like this, it is probably a mineral.

DOES IT HAVE A SPECIAL SHAPE? IS IT POINTY LIKE A SPIKE, OR CUBIC LIKE A BLOCK?

If you find something that has a very special shape, it is probably a mineral. Some minerals form in spikes or needles, and some take the form of cubes or six-sided barrels. Still others

GYPSUM These needle-like crystals are gypsum and can't be confused with any rock.

FELDSPAR Feldspar crystals often are blocky and have sharp edges, unlike rocks.

form in complex shapes with lots of little angles. Rocks don't form in these shapes.

FELDSPAR This feldspar chunk is normally dull, but at the right angle, it "flashes" in the light.

IS IT SHINY OR "FLASHY" ONLY WHEN YOU HOLD IT AT A CERTAIN ANGLE?

Some minerals have special structures inside them that make them appear shiny or lustrous when you hold them at certain angles. With these minerals, they appear to "flash" when you move them around under bright light. Try checking out minerals like feldspar on page 89 and calcite on page 80. Rocks won't show this flashiness unless these minerals are inside them, too.

Rock Collecting Basics

One of the best ways to build your rock and mineral collection is to learn to identify the most common kinds of rocks and then find examples of each of them. This section of the book includes some of the most well-known and interesting igneous, sedimentary, and metamorphic rocks. Some, such as granite or limestone, you might see used in buildings, statues, or even in your house. Others, such as skarn, are rare but equally as interesting and important to know about. Once you learn all about rocks, you can use that knowledge to find crystals and gems inside them!

When you start looking for rocks, you'll begin to notice that they are everywhere: along roads, in forests, on the beach. But you will quickly notice the differences between them, like how some rocks are very hard and others are softer and crumbly. Even pieces that seem to be the same rock might have some differences, such as their color. For example, granite is a kind of rock that is found all over the world, but it can be red, pink, white, or brown depending on where you find it. That can make identification a little tricky, so you'll have to learn how to spot a rock's most important traits.

WHERE TO LOOK

Rocks are great to collect because you can find them almost everywhere. Any place where weathering has exposed lots of rock is a great place to start, such as along rivers, lakes, and oceans. Areas with few plants, like deserts, are excellent places to look for rocks, and some of the most exciting rocks are found in mountainous areas. But mountains can be dangerous and take a lot of skill to search, so not everyone can hunt for rocks there. Wherever you look, you'll find rocks. Just be sure to be very careful wherever you go, always collect with an adult present, and never go out alone!

Range Maps for Common Rocks

Some North American rocks are found from Alaska to Mexico, while others are only found in certain areas. These maps show you the main areas where you're likely to find certain kinds of rocks.

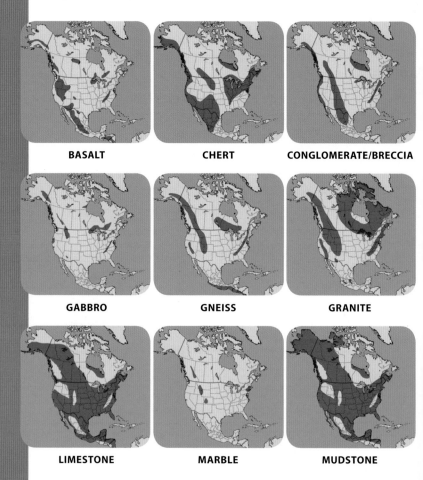

BASALT

CHERT

CONGLOMERATE/BRECCIA

GABBRO

GNEISS

GRANITE

LIMESTONE

MARBLE

MUDSTONE

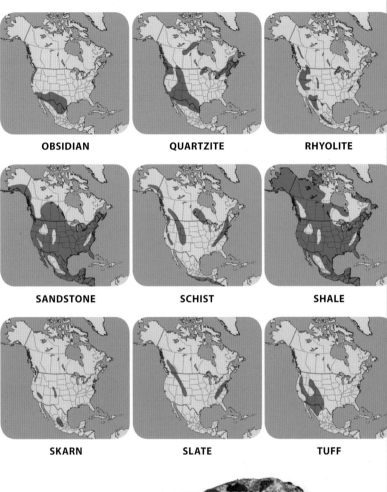

OBSIDIAN QUARTZITE RHYOLITE

SANDSTONE SCHIST SHALE

SKARN SLATE TUFF

Basalt *(say it, "buh-salt")*

Basalt is a dark, dense rock that formed when lava cooled very quickly. Basalt formed when a volcano erupted lava out onto the Earth. This lava had lots of iron in it, which helps make basalt dark colored. Basalt can also have lots of air bubbles in it, and minerals sometimes fill in those gaps.

Colors: Dark gray to black, but sometimes greenish or reddish.

Gabbro *(say it, "gab-ro")*

Gabbro is a dark and heavy rock. It formed when magma cooled off when it was still deep inside the Earth. This gives it a coarse, "chunky" look. Actually, gabbro forms from the same melted rock that basalt does. The difference is that basalt cooled very quickly on the surface but gabbro cooled slowly, deep underground.

Colors: Usually black, gray, brown, greenish, and yellowish.

Granite *(say it, "gran-it")*

Granite is a very common rock that formed deep underground when magma cooled very slowly. It has big grains of minerals that look like chunky colored spots. Sometimes the mineral grains have blocky crystal shapes, or they can be very shiny. Granite is also one of the most common rocks in the world, and you can find it all over the country.

Colors: Found in many colors; white, gray, black, brown, and pink are very common.

Obsidian *(say it, "obb-sid-ee-an")*

Obsidian is a special kind of glass that forms naturally. Normally, lava has a small amount of water in it, but obsidian forms from special lava that has almost no water in it at all. It is very brittle and will break just like glass. Its edges can be very sharp, so be careful. Thin pieces will also let light shine through them.

Colors: Usually black, but it can sometimes be gray or brown.

Rhyolite *(say it, "rye-oh-lite")*

Rhyolite is a dense, lighter-colored rock that formed when lava cooled very quickly. It's kind of like basalt but has much more quartz in it, which makes it lighter in color. It can have lots of air bubbles in it, as well as blocky crystals trapped inside it. Sometimes it can also have stripes of color. The stripes formed when the lava was still soft and moving.

Colors: Mostly gray or brown, but sometimes reddish.

Tuff

Tuff is a different kind of igneous rock. It forms when rock dust and ash are squished and then harden. In some kinds of volcanic eruptions, lots of dust and rock bits are thrown out with the lava. When all of that dust settles, it can harden together and form tuff. Sometimes tuff is soft and breaks easily, but it can also be very hard and almost like glass. You will mostly find tuff in dry, desert areas.

Colors: Commonly gray, but also brown and reddish brown.

Chert

Chert is a very hard rock that is interesting. It formed when the hard skeletons of microscopic lifeforms (so small that you can't see them) settled to the bottom of ancient seas and hardened. It can be found in all kinds of places, but it is easiest to find on beaches, where it often looks like shiny, rounded pebbles. It can also be rough with sharp edges.

Colors: Usually gray, brown, or tan; black chert is called flint.

Conglomerate (say it, "kon-glom-er-it")
Breccia (say it, "bresh-ee-uh")

BRECCIA

Conglomerate and breccia are two kinds of rocks that are made up of smaller rocks that are stuck together. Conglomerate formed in water and has rounded pebbles inside it. Breccia formed when an earthquake or volcano broke up rocks, so it has lots of jagged, pointy rock pieces inside it. In both kinds of rocks, in between the bigger pieces is a fine-grained material, kind of like cement.

Colors: Both are multicolored but mostly gray and brown.

CONGLOMERATE

Limestone (say it, "lime-stone")

Limestone is a soft, light-colored rock that formed when ancient coral reefs turned into rock. It used to be the bottom of the ocean! Sometimes it has fossil shells and coral within it. It can feel chalky when you touch it, and with an adult's help, you can make limestone fizz or bubble when you put vinegar on it.

Colors: Usually gray, brown, or yellowish, but it can also be very dark and almost black.

Mudstone *(say it, "mud-stone")*

As you might have guessed, mudstone forms from mud. When mud and clay collect at the bottom of a lake, they can harden over time to become mudstone. It has very fine grains of rocks and minerals in it. Mudstone is usually rough and gritty and can make your hands dusty.

Colors: Usually gray, tan, or brown.

Sandstone *(say it, "sand-stone")*

Sandstone is a rock that is made of sand that is stuck together. When sand settles at the bottom of a lake or sea, it can compact and harden. So sandstone looks and feels like hard sand. Sometimes it can have fossils, like snail shells, stuck inside of it, or it can have colored layers. It is often crumbly and gritty.

Colors: Often red, yellow, brown, tan, gray, or even multicolored.

Shale

Shale is a soft rock with lots of layers. It is made of mud and clay, just like mudstone. The main difference between them is that shale has many layers. Shale is a fun rock to find because you may find fossils between the layers. With an adult's help, you can use a thin tool or a knife to split the layers apart.

Colors: Usually gray, brown, tan, or yellowish.

Gneiss *(say it, "nice")*

Gneiss is a very common rock that forms when other rocks are heated up and pressed by lots of weight. This gives the rock lots of stripes of color. But it still looks a little bit like the original rock, too. For example, granite is a rock that can be turned into gneiss, and when it does it still looks a little bit like granite. In that case, we call it "granitic gneiss." There are lots of kinds of gneiss.

Colors: Gneiss can have many colors, but gray, white, black, brown, and green are common.

Marble

Marble is a special kind of metamorphic rock because it is mostly made up of a mineral called calcite. That makes marble fairly soft and often very white in color. It can also look very sparkly because of all the calcite crystals in it. Marble formed when lime-stone was changed by heat and pressure.

Colors: White, sometimes with some brown or black stains.

Quartzite *(say it, "kwarts-ite")*

Quartzite is a rock that formed from sandstone. When sandstone is affected by heat or certain chemicals, the grains of sand can start to merge together. This makes quartzite, which is named that because it is made primarily of the mineral quartz. It is a very hard rock that can sometimes look glassy or have stripes of color in it. It is often found on beaches as round pebbles.

Colors: Can be brown, gray, green, pink, and sometimes have stripes of other colors.

Schist *(say it, "shist")*

Schist is another common rock that forms when other rocks are exposed to lots of heat and pressure. This can change the rocks a lot and gives them many tightly packed layers. Schist is often flaky and some types break easily. It can also have gems, like garnet, trapped inside its layers.

Colors: Often gray, brown, or green and can have spots of other colors; many kinds of schist are very shiny and glittery.

Skarn

Skarn is a very interesting rock. It forms when hot magma underground rises up and touches other rocks, particularly limestone. This partially melts the rocks and puts other minerals into them. When the melted material cools, it forms a new chunky rock filled with crystals of colorful minerals, like garnets. Skarn isn't very common, but you might see it in some mountainous areas.

Colors: Can be a wide variety of different colors and is very sparkly; most is brown or green.

Slate

When shale and all of its many layers are squashed and heated, the layers get even tighter and harder. It also turns darker in color, too. This is called slate, and it is what school chalkboards used to be made of. It forms in big sheets that are very brittle. Its layers can be split apart to reveal smooth surfaces. It is most common in areas with mountains.

Colors: Dark gray or black, sometimes with some brown.

Mineral Collecting Basics

There are so many different minerals that it may seem impossible to tell them all apart, but it's actually a lot easier than you might think! Unlike rocks, which can look very different depending on where you find them, minerals have much more uniform traits. For example, a quartz crystal from California and one from New York will share the same hardness, the same shape, the same luster, and probably the same color. Even other minerals that have many different possible crystal shapes, such as calcite, will be easy to identify once you know their hardness, streak color, and other key traits—because no matter what crystal shape a calcite specimen may have, its other traits will be the same! Just always be sure to write down where you find each piece. This will help you later on. In the following pages, we'll look at some of the most common and important minerals and their distinguishing traits so that you can begin identifying them!

WHERE TO LOOK

Like rocks, minerals can be found everywhere. Every kind of rock is made up of little mineral grains, which often look like tiny flecks of color in the rock. Places like rivers and beaches are also great for finding rounded pebbles of quartz and other tough minerals, too. But most collectors look for nice crystals, and those are a lot rarer. When hunting for crystals, a good place to look is inside holes in rocks, where crystals may have had room to form. Holes and cracks

This hole in basalt has several kinds of crystals in it!

in rocks can hold crystals, big and small, or none at all! Lots of holes in rocks, especially limestone, may appear to sparkle—that's because there are hundreds of tiny crystals inside! Most of the time, these holes are revealed in places where rocks are weathering.

It's also important to remember that not all kinds of rocks may be hiding crystals inside them. Sandstone, for example, rarely grows any kind of crystals within it, but the spaces in limestone and basalt often do. So you can see that learning all about rocks will help you find minerals, too!

On the following pages, the most important minerals of all are marked with an asterisk (✱).

Range Maps for Common Minerals

The most common minerals in North America are shown here. Many have very wide ranges and are found all over, while others are only found in a few places. These maps will give you a basic idea of where to look for each.

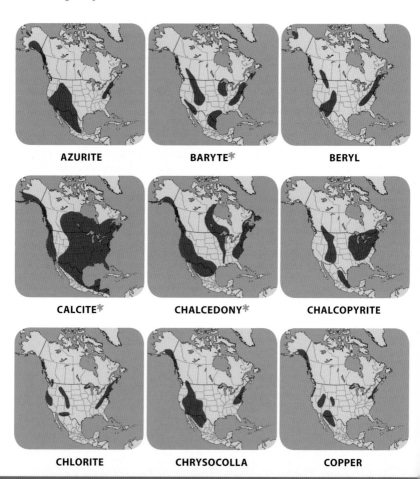

AZURITE

BARYTE✳

BERYL

CALCITE✳

CHALCEDONY✳

CHALCOPYRITE

CHLORITE

CHRYSOCOLLA

COPPER

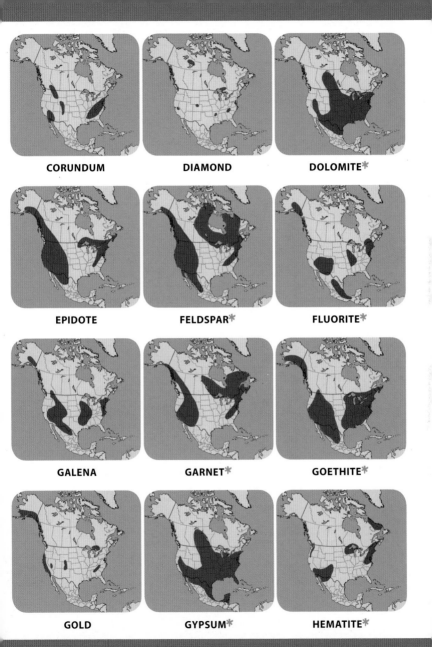

CORUNDUM

DIAMOND

DOLOMITE*

EPIDOTE

FELDSPAR*

FLUORITE*

GALENA

GARNET*

GOETHITE*

GOLD

GYPSUM*

HEMATITE*

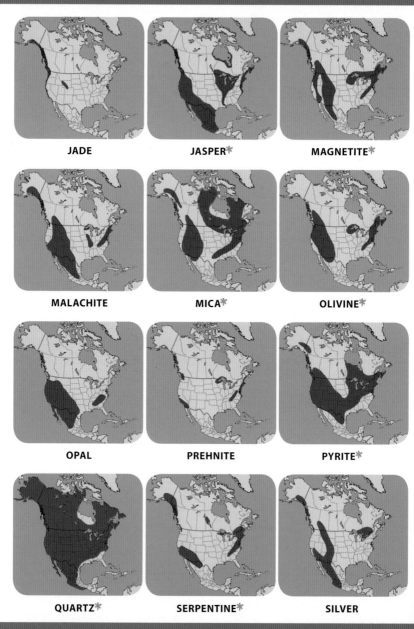

JADE

JASPER*

MAGNETITE*

MALACHITE

MICA*

OLIVINE*

OPAL

PREHNITE

PYRITE*

QUARTZ*

SERPENTINE*

SILVER

SPHALERITE

TALC

TOURMALINE

TURQUOISE

ZEOLITE

Beryl *(say it, "bare-ill")*

Streak color: colorless
Hardness: 7.5–8 (silicon carbide will scratch it)

- Beryl is a hard mineral that forms in igneous rocks.

- Beryl crystals are long with six sides and flat ends. Their sides have deep grooves in them. Normally you'll find crystals stuck in quartz or micas.

- It can have many colors, from gray to yellow. Green beryl is better known as emerald, and blue beryl is called aquamarine. These two colors are famous gems that you've probably heard of. Beryl is usually glassy.

- Beryl forms mostly in very coarse, chunky granite. Mountainous regions are some of the best places to find that kind of rock.

Calcite* *(say it, "kal-site")*

Streak color: white
Hardness: 3 (a U.S. nickel will scratch it)

- Calcite is another very common mineral, found nearly anywhere but especially in sedimentary rocks.

- Calcite forms in many, many different shapes. Its crystals can be very sharp and pointy with six sides, or it can look like a cube that has been squashed sideways. It can also often be found as white chunks.

- Usually white, but it can also be yellow or brown.

- When calcite breaks, the broken spot often looks very square, sometimes with little edges, like stair steps. This can help identify it.

Corundum *(say it, "cor-un-dum")*

Streak color: white
Hardness: 9 (silicon carbide will scratch it)

- Corundum is a very hard mineral that forms in metamorphic rocks.

- Corundum forms long, pointy, six-sided crystals, but it can also just be little round grains in rocks.

- It can have a variety of colors, but most are gray. The red or pink variety is called ruby, and the blue variety is called sapphire, and they are rare gemstones!

- Corundum is mostly found in metamorphic rocks like schist, but it can also be found in very coarse granite. It is most common in mountainous regions.

Diamond *(say it, "die-am-ond")*

Streak color: none
Hardness: 10 (only diamond will scratch it!)

- Diamonds are rare and valuable gemstones. They are almost always found inside a special and rare kind of rock called kimberlite.

- Diamonds are usually tiny specks, but some that grow big enough show a shape called an octahedron, which looks like two pyramids put bottom-to-bottom.

- They are usually white or clear, but some are gray, brown, or yellow; they are always very glassy.

- Unfortunately, diamonds are very hard to find, and you won't be able to find one unless you go to special mines that let you search for them. Most diamonds are very tiny and hard to see, and it takes lots of work to get one loose from rock.

Fluorite* *(say it, "flor-ite")*

Streak color: white
Hardness: 4 (a steel knife will scratch it)

- Fluorite is fairly common and forms in many different kinds of environments.

- Its most common crystal shape is a perfect cube, but it is also commonly found as rough masses.

- Fluorite is famous for its many colors; it can be green, purple, blue, pink, white, or have no color at all!

- It can be found in a variety of kinds of rocks, but it often appears in holes within sedimentary rocks, especially limestone.

Garnet* *(say it, "gar-net")*

Streak color: white or none
Hardness: 6.5–7.5 (a steel file will scratch it)

- Garnets are very common and found in all kinds of different areas.

- There are actually many different kinds of garnet. The most common are called almandine, andradite, and grossular. All of them form as small crystals shaped like balls with lots of little sides.

- Many garnets are brown, yellow, or red, and most are glassy.

- Garnets can mostly be found as grains inside rocks, like granite. You can also sometimes find them loose in the sand in rivers, but they will be very small.

Mica* *(say it, "my-ka")*

Streak color: colorless
Hardness: 2.5–3 (your fingernail could scratch it)

- There are many different mica minerals, and most are common, especially the ones called muscovite and phlogopite.

- Micas are usually found as crystals that are as thin and flaky as paper! They grow in stacks, just like the paper in a book, and you can even peel off individual crystals. They are flexible and can bend a lot before they break!

- They can be gray, black, brown, or yellow and are very see-through when thin. They can also be very lustrous and shiny, almost like metal.

- Most micas will be seen in rocks, especially speckled rocks like granite. Look for the flaky, shiny spots in rocks.

Olivine* *(say it, "olive-een")*

Streak color: colorless
Hardness: 6.5–7 (a steel file will scratch it)

- Olivine is very common, but normally it is so small you won't even notice it!

- When you see olivine, it will most often be as small grains with no crystal shape. Most pieces will be found in rocks, and you may need a magnifying glass to spot it.

- Olivine is usually green but can also be brown.

- Dark rocks, like gabbro and basalt, contain lots of olivine. You can also find it as little grains in sand. It may look a little boring, but olivine is a very important mineral in many parts of the Earth!

Opal *(say it, "ope-ul")*

Streak color: white
Hardness: 5.5–6.5 (porcelain will scratch it)

- Opal is a unique material because it has the same ingredients as quartz, but it is not actually a mineral! That's because opal does not form crystals, and for something to be a mineral it must form crystals.

- Opal is usually found as glassy chunks that fill the spaces in rocks.

- Its most common color is white, but it can actually be almost any color. Some rare opal has a special trait and will show flashes of rainbow colors when you move it around in bright light!

- Opal doesn't survive very well in wet climates, so it is best found in desert regions.

Prehnite *(say it, "pren-ite")*

Streak color: white
Hardness: 6–6.5 (porcelain should scratch it)

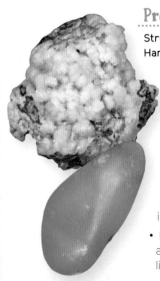

- Prehnite is a mineral that is not common everywhere and usually forms inside holes in certain rocks.

- Most of the time, you'll see prehnite as groups of little balls, like a bunch of grapes. But it can also be found as rounded pebbles on beaches.

- Prehnite is usually pale green, almost like a green apple, but it can also be gray or brownish. It is often glassy and a little see-through.

- Prehnite can be found in mountainous areas, as well as in regions with lots of dark rocks like basalt.

Quartz* *(say it, "kwarts")*

Streak color: none
Hardness: 7 (a steel file will scratch it)

- Quartz is the world's most common mineral and is found almost anywhere.

- Quartz forms in many different ways. Six-sided crystal points, big white masses, and little crusts of sparkly crystals are all common ways to find quartz. It is usually colorless or white but can be gray, yellow, brown, and other colors as well.

- It is most common as the white spots in granite and other rocks.

- You won't have any trouble finding quartz. Look for hard, white, glassy masses on beaches or along rivers.

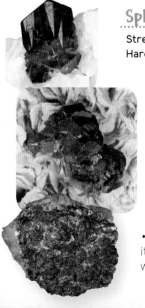

Sphalerite *(say it, "s-fal-er-ite")*

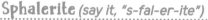

Streak color: light brown
Hardness: 3.5–4 (a pocket knife will scratch it)

- Sphalerite is an uncommon mineral that forms in sedimentary rocks. It contains zinc, a metal that we use in lots of things.

- Sphalerite crystals can be many different shapes. Most of its crystals are very complex and have many different angles and sides. Sometimes it is found just as dark, pointy lumps inside holes in rocks.

- It can be brown, yellow, red, black, or green and is usually very shiny.

- Sphalerite is found in many kinds of rocks, but it can be easiest to find inside holes in limestone where it is usually found with galena and calcite.

Tourmaline *(say it, "tor-ma-leen")*

Streak color: white
Hardness: 7-7.5 (a steel file might scratch it)

- Tourmaline is an uncommon gemstone that is usually found inside very coarse, chunky granite.

- Tourmaline is found as long crystals with grooved sides.

- There are several kinds of tourmaline, and the most common one (called schorl) is black, but other rarer ones can be pink, blue, or green and see-through. All of them are glassy.

- Tourmaline is found in coarse, rough rocks, so mountainous areas are best for finding it.

Zeolites *(say it, "zee-oh-lite")*

Streak color: white
Hardness: 3.5-5.5 (a pocket knife will scratch them)

- The zeolites are a big family of minerals that mostly form in the holes and cracks within dark rocks. When the rock weathers, it breaks down and its ingredients can turn into zeolites.

- Many zeolites form as tiny, thin crystals that look like needles. Lots of times, the needles are bunched together like a ball. This can make some zeolites look fuzzy.

- Most zeolites are white or colorless and glassy.

- Zeolites are mostly found in basalt, and since basalt is very common, that means many zeolites are common as well. Look inside the little holes in the rock for tiny white crystals. Many zeolites are found on beaches.

Azurite *(say it, "As-zhur-ite")*

Streak color: light blue
Hardness: 3.5-4 (a pocket knife will scratch it)

- Azurite is rare, and you can only find it in areas where copper is also found.

- Azurite can form as flat, pointy crystals that sometimes grow in clusters that look like flowers, but it can also be found as a lumpy crust on rocks

- It is always blue, but it can be dark blue to pale blue; it gets its color from the copper in it.

- Azurite is most common in dry, desert areas because it weathers quickly in wet areas. It is always found with other minerals that contain copper, such as malachite.

Baryte* *(say it, "bare-ite")*

Streak color: white
Hardness: 3-3.5 (a U.S. nickel will scratch it)

- Barite is uncommon, but it is found in many different kinds of places.

- It forms most commonly as crystals that look like thin blades; crystals are sometimes found in stacked groups and clusters.

- Barite is brittle and its crystals break easily. Barite crystals are sometimes colorless, but they can also be brown, tan, or even blue. They can be glassy, but most of the time they are dull.

- Blades of barite can be found in openings in different kinds of rocks, like limestone or rhyolite.

Chrysocolla
(say it, "kriss-oh-cole-ah")

Streak color: pale blue
Hardness: 2–4 (a U.S. nickel will usually scratch it)

- Chrysocolla might look a little like turquoise, but it's much more common and much softer.

- Chrysocolla does not form crystals; instead, it is found as crusts or masses on or in other rocks.

- It is always blue and sometimes light or dark colored. It usually has a dull luster. It can often be crumbly and dusty.

- Chrysocolla can be found anyplace that has copper. It can be best found in dry areas like deserts.

Dolomite* *(say it, "doh-loh-mite")*

Streak color: white
Hardness: 3.5–4 (a pocket knife will scratch it)

- Dolomite is a common mineral, but it is not always well formed, so it can be easy to overlook.

- When it forms crystals, they appear like little blocks that are leaning over, or they can also look like blocks that have curving sides. But it can also form as rough masses with no crystal shape.

- It is most often white or gray or sometimes tan or brown. It is usually glassy but can be dull as well.

- Dolomite is most common in sedimentary rocks, such as within holes in limestone or inside geodes.

Feldspars* *(say it, "feld-spar")*

Streak color: white
Hardness: 6–6.5 (porcelain may scratch it)

- Feldspar is very common and is found almost everywhere in the world!

- There are actually many different feldspars, and most form as blocky crystals. But all feldspars are most commonly found as grains in rocks, especially granite.

- Feldspars are often light colored, such as white, tan, or pink, but some can be very dark gray or greenish.

- Feldspar crystals are not common, and you probably won't find them, but feldspar is very common as chunks inside rocks and as pebbles. If you see light-colored spots in coarse rocks like granite, those are often feldspars.

Gypsum* *(say it, "jip-sum")*

Streak color: white
Hardness: 2 (a fingernail will scratch it)

- Gypsum is a very common mineral found in places like fields and deserts.

- Gypsum forms in a variety of ways. Many times it is found just as big, ugly masses, but sometimes its crystals are as clear as water.

- It can be colorless or white but is more often brown or gray. Crystals are glassy, but most of the time gypsum is very dull.

- Gypsum is best found in dry sedimentary areas, like deserts, and can be found in layers of limestone and other rocks.

Malachite *(say it, "mal-a-kite")*

Streak color: light green
Hardness: 3.5–4 (a pocket knife will scratch it)

- Malachite is uncommon, but you can find it anywhere there is copper.

- Malachite crystals are shaped like tiny needles, but malachite most often forms as crusts or chunks inside other rocks.

- Like many minerals that have copper in them, malachite is always green, but it can be dark or light green.

- Malachite is found in many places and in many kinds of rocks, but it survives best in dry areas. It can be found with copper and other minerals with copper in them, and inside rocks like basalt.

Turquoise *(say it, "turk-oiz")*

Streak color: pale green
Hardness: 5–6 (porcelain will scratch it)

- Turquoise is rare but very popular in jewelry.

- Turquoise is usually found as little masses or veins within cracks in rocks. It is usually lumpy, but if it is broken it can have very smooth surfaces.

- It is light to dark blue in color, sometimes with a green tint.

- It is only found in dry desert areas because it doesn't survive well in wetter regions. It can be found inside different kinds of rocks, but it is easy to spot if you're lucky enough to find it.

Chalcedony*
(say it, "kal-sed-oh-nee")

Streak color: white
Hardness: 6.5–7 (porcelain may scratch it)

- Chalcedony is very common and can be found all over, especially on beaches. It is a special kind of quartz.

- You won't find it as crystals, only as masses or pebbles with no specific shape.

- It can be nearly any color, but it is most often brown, red, and yellow, and sometimes multicolored. It usually has a waxy look, especially when rounded and smoothed by water.

- It is found in many places, but it is easiest to find on beaches and near rivers. It is also translucent, which means that it will let a little light shine through it, if it isn't too thick.

Chlorite (say it, "klor-ite")

Streak color: colorless to light green
Hardness: 2–2.5 (your fingernail will scratch it)

- Chlorite is very common, but it is usually dark and small, so it is easy to miss.

- Chlorite forms as tiny crusts on rocks or in holes in rocks, not often as crystals. Sometimes it can form as balls in rocks.

- It is almost always dark green, but sometimes it can be black or dark brown. It is mostly dull in luster but sometimes can look greasy.

- Chlorite is most commonly found along the inside of the spaces in dark volcanic rocks like basalt. It may seem uninteresting, but it is an important and common mineral.

Epidote *(say it, "ep-ih-dote")*

Streak color: white to gray
Hardness: 6–7 (a steel file will scratch it)

- Epidote is a common mineral because it can form when other rocks and minerals are weathering.

- Epidote is often found as a crust on top of rocks, but it can also form little flat crystals inside holes in rocks.

- It is most often yellow-green, and its color can help identify it.

- Epidote forms in many places and in many rocks, particularly granite and basalt.

Jade *(say it, "jayd")*

Streak color: white
Hardness: 5–6 (porcelain will scratch it)

- Jade is the name for green gemstones that are often found on the Pacific coast. But it isn't just one mineral; it is actually a mixture of green minerals.

- Jade is most often found as rounded pebbles on shores, and beaches are the best place to look for it.

- It is usually green but can be very dark. Some kinds are nearly white. The best pieces of jade are a little translucent, which means that a little light will shine through them if they aren't too thick. Rounded pebbles have a waxy luster.

- Jade is very collectible as loose pebbles on Pacific beaches, but it is not common.

Jasper* *(say it, "jass-per")*

Streak color: none
Hardness: 6.5–7 (a steel file will scratch it)

- Jasper is very common and can be found almost anywhere in gravel and on beaches.

- Jasper doesn't form as crystals and instead can only be found as chunks or pebbles.

- It can be any color, but it is most often brown, red, or yellow. If it's broken, it can be very dull, but if it is rounded and smoothed in water, it can look shiny and waxy.

- Jasper is found in many places, but it is easiest to find on beaches and near rivers where the water makes it rounded, smooth, and shiny.

Serpentine* *(say it, "ser-pen-teen")*

Streak color: white to green
Hardness: 2.5–4 (a pocket knife will scratch it)

- Serpentine is not very common and only forms in certain areas, such as near mountains.

- It forms as big masses, not as crystals, and often has grooves on its surfaces.

- Serpentine is usually dark green, sometimes with some tan or black coloration. It is opaque, which means it is not see-through.

- Serpentine has a unique feel—when you touch it, it feels greasy or slippery!

- Serpentine is often found near coasts and in mountain areas, where there is a lot of tectonic plate movement!

Talc*

Streak color: white
Hardness: 1 (your fingernail will scratch it)

- Talc is not very common, but it can be found in areas with lots of metamorphic rocks, such as mountainous regions.

- Talc usually forms in small masses, not as crystals.

- It is often light colored, sometimes white but more often green. Thin pieces can be a little bit see-through.

- Talc is the softest mineral of all! You can very easily scratch it with your fingernails, and it feels very slippery to the touch, almost like soap! Many pieces are also very flaky and glittery.

Chalcopyrite *(say it, "kal-co-pie-rite")*

Streak color: green-black
Hardness: 3.5–4 (a pocket knife will scratch it)

- Chalcopyrite is a metallic mineral that looks a lot like pyrite, but it is not quite as common and is softer than pyrite.

- Chalcopyrite crystals are shaped like little triangles or wedges with lots of tiny grooves, but it is more often found as rough chunks inside holes in rocks.

- It is often yellow or orange and metallic, but it can also have a purple or blue look.

- Chalcopyrite is mostly found inside sedimentary rocks, especially limestone. It is often seen with sphalerite.

Copper

Streak color: coppery
Hardness: 2.5–3 (a U.S. nickel will scratch it)

- Copper is a metal that we use for many things.

- Copper is mostly found as rough masses inside rocks, but it can also form crystals. Crystals can be all kinds of shapes, from little blocks to shapes that look like branches.

- Copper is orange-red and metallic, but it is very often weathered, which makes it look blue or green. The blue and green color is just on the surface of the copper and can be scratched away. The blue and green is actually other minerals, such as malachite and chrysocolla!

- Certain volcanic rocks, like basalt, are places where it often forms. Look for bright green or blue colors in rocks because it can mean that copper is nearby!

Galena *(say it, "guh-lee-nah")*

Streak color: gray
Hardness: 2.5 (a U.S. nickel will scratch it)

- Galena is a heavy metallic mineral that mostly contains lead; it can be common if you're in the right environment. **But lead can be dangerous, so only handle it with gloves on!**

- Galena can be found as crystals that look like cubes or blocks. It can also be found as chunks with no special shape, but when you break a chunk, it will actually break into block shapes!

- It is gray and metallic, but sometimes it can look dull if it is weathered. If you freshly break a piece, it will be very shiny. It is also very heavy, and even a small piece will feel hefty.

- Galena is most often found inside holes in limestone.

Goethite* *(say it, "ger-tite")*

Streak color: yellow-brown
Hardness: 5–5.5 (a pocket knife will scratch it)

- Goethite is another very common mineral that is comprised mostly of iron and is found all over. It forms when other minerals with iron in them weather away.

- Crystals are rare; most of the time you'll just find it as little crumbly chunks or as rusty coatings on other rocks and minerals.

- Goethite is black and metallic, but usually it is weathered, which makes it a rusty yellow-brown color and very dusty.

- Goethite is found all over, but it isn't always exciting. Any time you see a rusty yellow stain or crust on other rocks or minerals, you can guess that it's goethite.

Gold

Streak color: gold
Hardness: 2.5 (a U.S. nickel will scratch it)

- Gold is a rare metal that has been used for jewelry and as money for thousands of years.

- Gold is most often found as little flecks or grains in rocks and especially in quartz. Little grains or nuggets can be found in some rivers.

- It is always bright yellow and metallic. Gold is special because it does not change color, no matter how weathered it gets!

- Gold is very hard to find, especially because most pieces are so tiny. It is mostly found in mountainous areas.

Hematite* *(say it, "hee-mah-tite")*

Streak color: red-brown
Hardness: 5–6 (porcelain will scratch it)

- Hematite is a very common mineral that is made primarily of iron, and it is found in all kinds of places.

- If it is crystallized, hematite looks like tiny blades, but usually it forms as chunky masses or layers.

- Hematite is usually black and metallic, but if it is weathered, it can have a dusty reddish color that makes your hands dirty.

- Hematite can be found almost anywhere! Big masses aren't very common except at mines, but any time you see a red dusty stain on another rock or mineral, it is usually caused by hematite.

Magnetite* *(say it, "mag-nah-tite")*

Streak color: black
Hardness: 5.5–6.5 (porcelain will scratch it)

- Magnetite is a mineral that is made up mostly of iron and can be found in many different kinds of rocks. It is magnetic and sticks to a magnet!

- You will find most magnetite as little grains or chunks inside rocks, especially dark rocks. But you could find tiny crystals, too; they form in a shape called an octahedron, which has eight faces that are shaped like bottom-to-bottom pyramids.

- It is usually black and metallic, but it turns brown when it weathers.

- Magnetite can be found in most dark-colored rocks as tiny grains. But you can also put a magnet in most sand or gravel, especially on beaches, and find pieces sticking to the magnet.

Pyrite* *(say it, "pie-rite")*

Streak color: dark green-gray
Hardness: 6–6.5 (porcelain will scratch it)

- Pyrite is a common mineral that is very popular and fun to collect; it can be found in all kinds of rocks.

- Pyrite crystals most commonly look like cubes or blocks, but it can also form as rough chunks.

- It is usually yellow or brass-colored and metallic; some people call it "fool's gold" because it kind of looks like gold. If it gets weathered, it can turn brown and dull.

- Pyrite can be found in all kinds of rocks. If you ever see a metallic, shiny, gold-colored mineral in limestone or shale, you can assume it is pyrite because it is so common.

Silver

Streak color: silvery
Hardness: 2.5–3 (a U.S. nickel will scratch it)

- Silver is a rare, valuable metal. It is used in jewelry and electronics.

- Silver is mostly found as little grains or chunks inside rocks and certain minerals, like quartz.

- When fresh and clean, silver is bright silvery white in color. But silver changes color easily when in the air, and it darkens and turns gray or black. Most natural silver will be dark when you find it, but it will still look metallic.

- Silver is rare. Most pieces will be very small and are found in rocks that are usually only in mines. Unfortunately, you probably won't find any silver yourself.

MINERALS FOUND MOSTLY IN ROCKS

Not all minerals can be found as loose pieces or as nice crystals. Certain minerals are almost always seen as little grains or chunks inside rocks. Some of these minerals are very common, but most people don't collect them because they don't look for them. Next time you find a colorful rock with lots of colored spots, such as granite, look for some of these minerals:

Amphiboles
(say it, "am-feh-bowl")

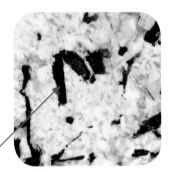

This is another large family of minerals, and the amphibole minerals are usually black or brown and often in long shapes. Sometimes they can look fibrous. You'll see lots of these in lighter rocks, like granite.

The long black grains in this granite are amphibole minerals.

Apatite *(say it, "app-ah-tite")*

Apatite is a glassy mineral that is mostly seen in coarse-grained rocks. It is usually little yellow, blue, green, or brown grains, but sometimes they can be long crystals. You'll mostly see these in metamorphic rocks.

This long blue crystal is apatite inside marble.

Feldspars *(say it, "feld-spar")*

We already talked about feldspars on page 89, but they are most common as grains and crystals in rocks, so that is how you will usually see them. Most are white or brown, and they can be blocky-shaped or needle-shaped. They can be very glassy.

The long, yellowish grains in this rhyolite are feldspar crystals.

Ilmenite *(say it, "ill-meh-nite")*

Ilmenite is a metallic mineral that has titanium and iron in it. It is often found as tiny grains in dark-colored rocks like gabbro and basalt. If you use a magnifying glass, you can see that ilmenite grains are sometimes a little blue in color. They are also slightly magnetic.

This tiny blue-black grain in gabbro is ilmenite

Micas *(say it, "my-kah")*

You can find mica minerals on their own (page 83), but they are most common as grains in rocks, so that's how you'll mostly find them. They look like gray or brown spots that are very flaky and shiny.

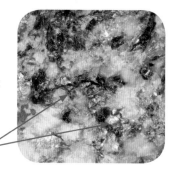

These shiny brown flakes are mica minerals in granite.

Olivine *(say it, "aw-lah-veen")*

We talked about olivine already on page 83, but most olivine is seen as tiny yellow grains in rocks. They are very easy to overlook, but if you look closely with magnification, you'll find lots of glassy, greenish-yellow grains in rocks like gabbro.

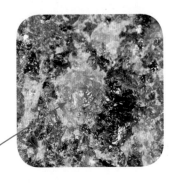

This green grain in gabbro is olivine.

Pyroxenes
(say it, "pie-rock-seen")

This is a large family of minerals, and all the pyroxene minerals are usually glassy and black, sometimes with blocky shapes. You'll see lots of these in dark rocks like gabbro.

The glassy black grains in this gabbro are pyroxene minerals.

Now that you know some of the minerals that mostly only appear as grains in rocks, see if you can spot some of them in this piece of granite! There are grains of orange feldspar, gray feldspar, black pyroxene, some thin brown mica, and white quartz— and those are just the ones big enough to see!

Agates, Fossils, and Dyed Crystals

There are lots of popular rocks and minerals that people like to collect. Some, like gold and diamonds, are more popular than others but can be very rare. But there are others that are just as popular that are easier to find and even easier to buy at a rock shop! Agates, thunder eggs, geodes, fossils, and fluorescent minerals are all special kinds of rocks and minerals that you will see in many shops. Since not all rocks and minerals can be found in every area, sometimes buying a specimen is the only way you can get one. And we'll also show you which dyed minerals to watch out for!

RARE AND POPULAR COLLECTIBLES

There are lots of rocks and minerals out there to collect, but unfortunately some are very rare and you probably won't get a chance to find them yourself. This includes rare fossils of extinct animals and minerals that glow different colors under special light. Some other minerals may be common but aren't always pretty until they are cut and polished, which you also may not be able to do yourself. But that's OK because many rock shops sell the rocks and minerals that are hard

A rare fossil animal nick-named a "Sea Scorpion" in shale.

to find! They also often sell specimens that have already been cut and polished for you. Many collectors buy specimens, and it is a great way to add neat treasures to your collection that you couldn't get any other way. Some very popular collectibles, such as agates and geodes, can actually be very common finds if you're in the right place. Because of this, lots of shops sell common rocks and minerals in both natural and polished forms, and it can be interesting to compare them.

Before you visit a rock shop, it's helpful to know a little about the neat rocks, minerals, and fossils that you're likely to see when you visit one.

This mineral called willemite is boring in normal light, but under ultraviolet light it glows green.

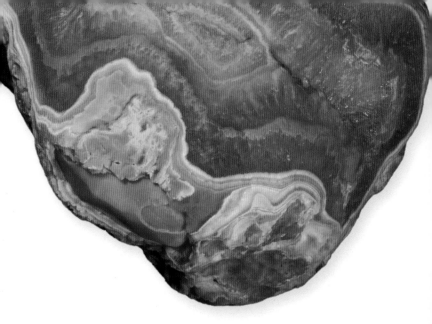

Agates (say it, "ag-it")

- Agates are an uncommon and mysterious type of mineral. They are made of layers of chalcedony (page 91), but no one knows exactly how they form!

- Agates form as nodules, which are rounded balls that grow inside spaces within rocks. From the outside, the nodules don't look like anything special, but when they're cut open they reveal the amazing ring-like bands that agates are famous for!

- Agates can be lots of different colors, but gray, brown, red, and yellow are common. They have rough, dull outsides but waxy insides.

- Agates are very hard, and it takes a very hard tool, like a file, to scratch them.

- Agates are most easily found on beaches or in rivers where weathering has broken them open to reveal their bands.

This green ball is actually an agate stuck in gray rock.

When cut and polished it shows amazing rings!

This weird gray ball is also an agate, but you can't see the rings until it's cut!

Thunder eggs

- Thunder eggs are a special kind of agate that are somewhat rare.

- They are agates that have formed inside a ball of rock. Their outside surfaces are rocky and rough, but their insides show the ring-like bands of an agate. If they are not broken, it can be tricky to identify one!

- Their exteriors can be gray or brown, just like other rocks. But the interior banding can be gray, brown, red, and yellow, like other kinds of agates.

- Most kinds of thunder eggs are found in drier areas, such as deserts. They can be tough to find, but look for round, lumpy rocks and then have an adult help you break or cut them!

This lumpy rock is actually hiding a thunder egg inside!

When a thunder egg is cut and polished, you can see the bands inside it.

Geodes
(say it, "jee-ode")

- Geodes are a very fun collectible, but they are only common in certain areas.

- Geodes are round balls of rock that are hollow inside! Many times they contain crystals, especially quartz crystals. But the outsides just look like round rocks, so they can be hard to spot.

- Their outsides are often brown, gray, or yellow, but their insides can be different colors depending on what crystals may be inside.

This is what a geode looks like when it is whole.

• You can't find geodes just anywhere. They form inside sedimentary rocks, especially limestone and shale, where they look like round balls. Sometimes they fall out and can be found loose. But they can be tricky to find and identify until you break them open to see what's inside!

And when it's broken, it can have crystals inside!

FLUORESCENT MINERALS

Some minerals have a very interesting trait: they can glow different colors in a special kind of light! These are called **fluorescent minerals**. If you have a type of lamp called an ultraviolet light, you can shine it on some minerals in the dark and they will glow. Ultraviolet light causes a reaction called fluorescence inside the mineral, and that reaction creates visible glowing light.

Not all minerals will fluoresce (glow) under an ultraviolet light, but the ones that do often glow in a completely different color than their normal color!

Here are some examples:

This reddish mica glows yellow-green!

This white opal glows bright green!

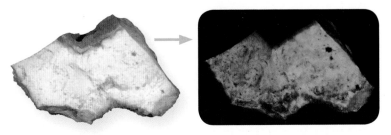

This rock contains a rare mineral called turneaureite (which is hard to say!), and you can't really see it normally, but under ultraviolet light it glows bright orange!

Minerals like calcite, fluorite, and apatite are also very often fluorescent. If you have an adult help you, you can get an ultraviolet light and shine it on rocks and minerals and see what glows! Be sure to do it in a dark room to see it well!

A safety note: Ultraviolet lights can be harmful to eyes and can also cause sunburn. When using a UV light, have an adult present, never look into the light, and don't shine it on your skin.

FOSSILS

Fossils are amazing surprises that you can find in some rocks. They are remains of ancient plants and animals that have turned into stone. Many fossils show us the shapes of plants and animals that are now extinct. But how did that happen?

Normally, when plants and animals die, their bodies rot away and disappear. But if the plant or animal body gets buried in mud and sediment, it won't rot entirely. Instead, it can stay in the mud for a very long time. Millions of years ago, this happened to lots of things that died, and their bodies became trapped in many layers of mud and sediments. As those layers slowly turned into sedimentary rocks like shale and limestone, the bodies of the plants and animals also turned into rock.

The process of plants and animals turning into rock is very slow. It happens when water makes the minerals in the mud interact with the chemicals in the plant or animal body. That creates new minerals that preserve the shape of the plant or animal!

Some of the most common fossils are plants, like ferns, or animal shells, such as snail or clam shells. More exciting fossils, such as dinosaurs and lizards, are very rare. When looking for fossils, you'll only find them in sedimentary rocks. Limestone, sandstone, and especially shale are the best places to look. You can even have an adult help split apart the layers of shale with a knife to see if anything is hiding in between them!

Petrified wood is fossilized wood, and sometimes there is so much preserved detail that you can even see tree bark, branches, and tree rings! Petrified wood is common, especially in desert areas and even on some beaches.

Coral fossils are very common all over the world. They often look like tubes or branches with a texture kind of like fabric. This type is called **horn coral** because it has the shape of a horn!

Since the soft parts of animals don't fossilize very well, it is often only their hard parts that we find. **Snail shells** are a perfect example! They were already hard and sturdy when the snails made them, so they often turned into fossils easily.

Just like snail shells, the shells of shellfish like clams, oysters, and scallops were also easily fossilized. This **scallop shell** is in sandstone and was found on a beach!

115

Other hard parts of animals, such as bones and especially teeth, are also often found as fossils. This tooth is from a small **shark**.

Some of the most exciting fossils are those of animals that no longer live on the Earth! This weird creature is called a **trilobite**, and they lived for hundreds of millions of years in the oceans. But today, they are extinct, and we can only see them in rocks. This one is in shale and was found in New York.

Since many fossils formed at the bottom of lakes and seas, it makes sense that **fossil fish** bones are very common. They are often very well preserved. Many times you can see the entire fish and even count its bones! They are common in shale and are found in between the layers in the rock.

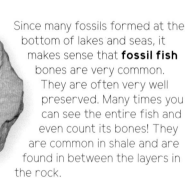

Soft parts of plants, such as their leaves, did not fossilize easily because they rot too quickly. But sometimes when they were buried very quickly in mud or volcanic ash, their shapes were preserved. This **leaf** from Colorado is in shale that formed when a whole forest was buried by a volcano!

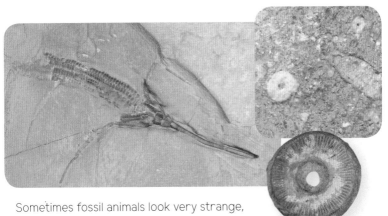

Sometimes fossil animals look very strange, and it can be hard to know what you are looking at! **Crinoids** are a type of animal that still live in oceans today, but long ago they were very common. They look like weird flowers with a long stem. Their stems often fell apart as they died, so you can find the pieces as strange circles in limestone. Those are pieces of a crinoid. They are very common, so keep an eye out!

In some parts of the world, you can find bugs trapped in amber. **Amber** is the preserved sap from ancient trees. When the sticky sap was flowing out of a tree long ago, any bug that touched it would get stuck. Some bugs got totally covered in sap, so when the sap dried out and hardened, the bug was preserved inside. Amber is not something you can find just anywhere, but it can show us an amazing look at ancient life!

NATURAL STONES COMMONLY FOUND IN ROCK SHOPS

There are many kinds of stones you'll see in stores, many of which are polished or cut. Some of the most frequently seen naturally colored stones are:

LAPIS LAZULI
A blue and white rock.

UNAKITE
A green and orange type of granite.

BRAZILIAN AGATES
Agates from Brazil, usually polished.

TIGER'S EYE
A yellow rock with lustrous fibers in it.

GYPSUM ROSE
A unique flower-like form of gypsum.

AVENTURINE
Quartzite that is naturally green because of micas in it.

SELENITE
A fiber-like form of gypsum.

AMAZONITE
A naturally blue-green feldspar.

SAND CALCITE
Calcite crystals that formed in sand.

JASPER
Colorful jasper, often polished.

COLORED CALCITE
Shiny calcite in vivid colors.

CRAZY LACE
A popular type of agate from Mexico.

"APACHE TEARS"
A type of obsidian nugget from the Southwestern U.S.

BLOODSTONE
A type of green chalcedony with bright red dots of color.

AMMONITES
Coiled shell fossils from an ancient squid-like animal.

ORTHOCERAS
Straight shell fossils from an ancient squid-like animal.

DYED STONES COMMONLY FOUND IN ROCK SHOPS

Shops also often have lots of dyed stones. Here are just a few commonly seen examples. For more, see page 120.

"TURQUESITE"
Dyed howlite (howlite is normally white).

YELLOW "OBSIDIAN"
Manmade glass.

BISMUTH CRYSTALS
Grown in a lab.

BLUE "OBSIDIAN"
Manmade glass.

AQUA AURA or TITANIUM QUARTZ
Quartz coated in titanium.

GREEN "OBSIDIAN"
Manmade glass.

GOLDSTONE or GOLDSHEEN
Manmade.

OPALITE
Manmade glass.

DYED MINERALS

In many rock shops and other stores, you might find some very pretty rocks for sale. Many have been cut and polished to make them more appealing, but some have even been dyed or had their colors changed so that they will sell better. When you are building your collection, you should be aware of things that have been changed just so they will sell. (They aren't really found like that in nature.) Here are some common examples.

Dyed agates

Many agates from Brazil are small and have very little color —most are gray. To make them sell better, they are dyed in very bright shades of pink, green, blue, and purple. These are often very cheap and pretty, but they are not natural.

Dyed quartz

Since quartz is the most common mineral on Earth, there is so much of it that small, broken pieces are not very valuable. To make some of it sell better, it is dyed just like agates, in pink, blue, green, and purple colors. Again, it is important to know that these colors are not natural.

"Citrine" *(say it, "sih-treen")*

Citrine is a form of quartz that is yellow in color, but natural citrine is very hard to find and is usually expensive. But if you heat up purple amethyst, which is more common, it will turn yellow-ish! Many shops sell inexpensive samples of this heated "citrine." Real citrine is very yellow, but heated amethyst is more yellow-brown or honey colored.

"Peacock ore"

Sometimes you'll find a metallic mineral for sale that has all kinds of blue, purple, and pink colors. It can be very pretty, and it is often sold with the name "peacock ore." This mineral is actually chalcopyrite, and those colors can happen naturally, but not very often. To make plain chalcopyrite worth more money, it is put in an acid that forces the colors to appear quickly.

"Magnetic hematite"

You may have seen some very strong magnets being sold that are black and shiny. Sometimes these are called "magnetic hematite," but that name is wrong. Natural hematite is not magnetic, and these shiny black magnets are actually manmade! They are also so strong that they can be dangerous (they can pinch skin and can lead to death if swallowed), so be careful with them.

Strange names

There are lots of interesting rocks in the world that can be polished to make them prettier. Sometimes these rocks are given names that make them more appealing to buy, like "zebra marble," "Dalmatian rock," and "spiderweb jasper." Many times, these are just made up names to make the rocks sound more appealing. If you want to know what kind of rock or mineral those things really are, ask the shop owner. And if they don't know, then you'll have to do some research of your own!

"Leopard jasper"

"Zebra marble"

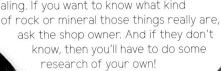

"Dalmatian rock"

"Rainforest jasper"

There are many ways that sellers can make rocks and minerals more appealing to buyers, but sometimes those ways can confuse collectors. Be careful about what you buy so that you are not fooled by bright colors or made-up names!

Stone beads are often found in rock shops and are a fun way to wear polished rocks and minerals. Sometimes they can be dyed different colors, too, so be sure to ask the store owner about them.

Frequently Asked Questions about Rock Collecting

Starting a rock collection should be fun! It's exciting to pick up cool pieces and compare them and learn their differences in a hands-on way. But you may end up with some questions, too. Like, what do you do with your collection? And, how do you polish neat stones that you've found? In this section, we'll answer some of these questions for you. But for others, you'll find the answer yourself as you build your rock and mineral collection!

WHERE TO BEGIN

When you want to begin collecting rocks and minerals, there's a lot to know first. What tools and safety equipment to bring, when to go looking, and how to stay safe are all very important things to consider.

STORAGE AND LABELING

One of the most important parts of starting a rock and mineral collection is keeping it safe and recording where you find each piece. You'll probably want some kind of box for your collection, and you want to keep your pieces from banging into each other. It's often best to get a box with little compartments, like a fishing tackle box. This way, each of your specimens can have a safe spot.

However you decide to store your collection, label each piece with exactly where you find the specimen, even if you don't know what it is yet. The location can help you identify the rock or mineral and can help you learn about the area's geology. A label with the location is also important to other collectors, if you ever show or trade specimens with other rock hounds! Recording where you find a rock is an essential part to becoming a successful collector and young geologist.

WHY DO PEOPLE COLLECT ROCKS AND MINERALS?

People collect rocks and minerals for many reasons. Some people do it because the pieces they collect are beautiful. Others do it because they like to learn about what they picked up. And others do it because they like to keep a souvenir from where they've been.

WHERE CAN I LOOK FOR ROCKS AND MINERALS? IS IT OK TO DO EVERYWHERE?

The best part about rock and mineral collecting is that you can find them almost anywhere! As long as you are in a natural space, you can probably find some neat rocks or pretty mineral specimens.

Some places are better than others, though. Good places to look include shorelines of lakes and near rivers, in forests, and even along dirt roads. Any place there is moving water can have a lot of rocks to pick up and examine. If you live near a desert, then you already know there are neat rocks all around for you to look at. And if you live near mountains, ask your parents to take you on a hike to look for rocks on the hillsides! But before you collect anything, keep safety in mind. Wild places can be very dangerous, so be careful and stay with an adult! Never go into moving water (such as rivers) because it can be moving very fast and sweep you away. And never go near cliffs or big rock piles because they can fall on you!

It is also very important to understand that you are **not** allowed to collect rocks everywhere. Many places are protected by the state or local government. This includes national parks, many state parks, national monuments, and Native American reservations. It is illegal to collect anything in these places! You also can't collect on private property without getting permission to do so first. (That's against the law.)

If you aren't sure if you can collect rocks and minerals where you are, always ask an adult to help you find out. To find public land where you can collect rocks legally, check your state's natural resources agency or department of natural resources. Rock collecting is allowed on some federal land, too. Visit the Bureau of Land Management (blm.gov) or the U.S. Forest Service (www.fs.fed.us) for more information. When in doubt, contact a nearby rock shop or a state field guide for advice.

WHAT SHOULD I BRING FOR ROCK COLLECTING?

There are a few things you should bring when you go rock collecting. Some things will make collecting easier, and others will keep you safe.

You should bring:

- ☐ Gloves, because some rocks can be sharp.

- ☐ A small shovel or trowel, for digging.

- ☐ A notebook and a pencil, to write down where you found your rocks.

- ☐ Water, both to rinse your specimens and to drink, especially if it's hot out.

- ☐ Sunblock lotion, to protect your skin from sunburn.

- ☐ A hat, to protect your eyes and face from the sun.

- ☐ Sturdy shoes, to protect your feet from sharp or falling rocks.

☐ A backpack, to hold your supplies and your rocks.

☐ A mobile phone, to call for help if you need to.

☐ A map or GPS system so you don't get lost.

☐ Some paper towels, to wrap up fragile specimens.

☐ A magnifying glass, to look at small specimens.

But always remember to **NEVER GO OUT ALONE**. When you are out having fun collecting rocks, you can easily get lost. Never leave home without a parent or other adult, and **ALWAYS** tell other people where you are going.

HOW DO I STAY SAFE WHEN ROCK COLLECTING?

Sometimes going out rock collecting can be an adventure, taking you to faraway places. But whether you are in your backyard or at the beach, you always want to stay safe by following these guidelines:

- Never, ever go alone. If you get lost or hurt, no one will be there to help you. So always ask an adult to come with you.

- Always bring a map, a charged smart phone, or a GPS system so that you do not get lost. A smart phone will also let you call for help if you need to.

- Always bring water to drink. It is very dangerous to be outside all day with no water!

- Never go into rivers, lakes, or oceans because even if the water looks calm it may actually be moving very fast.

- Never collect on or near a busy road.

- Never go near cliffs. If you are on top of one, it could easily crumble and make you fall. Or, if you are below one, it could fall on top of you.

- If a rock that you want is out of reach, you should just leave it. Never do anything risky to get a rock. Your safety is more important than the rock!

- Never go onto private property. This means that someone else owns the land. If you see signs that say "no trespassing," then you should turn around right away!

- Some rocks and minerals can be dangerous to collect. Never taste rocks and always wash your hands after rock collecting. If your hands are dirty, don't touch your face or eyes.

- Make sure you stay away from potentially dangerous animals and plants; this includes everything from snakes or alligators to cactus and poison ivy.

WHEN IS THE BEST TIME TO GO ROCK COLLECTING?

Some times of the day are better for collecting rocks than others. If it's too early or late in the day you might not have enough light to see. You also don't want to go out too late because when it gets dark you won't be able to find your way back. Midday is good because you'll have plenty of sunlight and lots of time. But if you live in a desert region, try earlier in the morning, before it gets too hot.

WHAT SHOULD I LOOK FOR?

Look for anything that appeals to you! If you think something is cool or pretty, then pick it up and write down where you found it. You should also look for unusual things. If you find a rock that is different from everything else around, you might have found something rare! Just always remember to make a note of where you found it. This will help you identify it later.

HOW DO I IDENTIFY THE THINGS I FOUND?

Many, but not all, rocks and minerals can be identified using this book. If you can't find your rock in this book, try looking in another rock book, or have an adult help you look on the internet. If you're having trouble on your own, try asking a teacher, or send a letter/email and photo to a museum where experts can help you.

When trying to identify your specimen, take note of these things: its color, its shape, how hard it is, how shiny it is, and where you found it. All of those things can help you learn more about it, no matter whether it is a rock or mineral.

WHAT CAN I DO WITH MY COLLECTION?

A collection is for your enjoyment, so the best thing you can do is show it to your friends and family. Share your stories of how and where you found each piece! Be sure to always keep a label with each piece that tells where it was found, even if you don't know what the rock is yet. You can always identify it later, but you might forget where you found it before you do! The location where a rock or mineral is found is very important for collectors.

ARE SOME ROCKS WORTH MONEY?

Some rocks and minerals, such as gold, rubies, and emeralds, can be worth lots of money. But those things are also very rare. The rocks you pick up on the beach or at the park are usually very common and not valuable. Even when very pretty, most rocks are not usually worth much at all.

Even though some rare minerals can be worth a lot of money, that is not the most important part of collecting. You should collect because you enjoy it, not because you want money. Collecting rocks and labeling them is a way to do science, and it will help you learn about the Earth beneath your feet.

WHAT IF I WANT TO POLISH WHAT I FOUND?

Cutting, polishing, and drilling rocks and minerals is a lot of fun because you can make a piece prettier or even turn it into jewelry. But remember that rocks and minerals are often very hard, and you need very special equipment to polish and cut stones. Some of the equipment can be very expensive, especially saws. But there is a good solution for young collectors: rock tumblers.

A rock tumbler is a machine with a small barrel. You put rocks into it, along with water and polishing grit, and it turns around slowly. After a few weeks, the rocks you put inside will begin to become shiny and polished! Rock tumblers take a lot of patience, and not everything you put into them will polish well. Lots of soft rocks and minerals will just break up and turn to dust, but hard minerals, like quartz, will get very shiny.

Rock tumblers can be bought at rock shops or on the internet. Have an adult help you find one, and be sure to follow the directions very carefully. With some time and effort, you can polish up the stones you find!

Glossary

BAND An easy-to-see layer in a rock or mineral.

BRECCIA A rock made up of broken pieces of other rocks that are stuck together.

COARSE Coarse rocks have mineral grains in them that are easy to see.

CONGLOMERATE A rock made up of rounded pebbles that are stuck together.

CRUST The hard, rocky outside of the Earth; the Earth's surface. This is where we live and where we find rocks.

CRYSTAL A solid shape formed when a mineral hardens. Each mineral has a different crystal shape.

CUBE A crystal shape that looks like a square block.

DULL A mineral that is not very shiny.

EARTHY A mineral that is not shiny at all and looks dusty or dirty.

EROSION When rocks or minerals wear (erode) away because of weathering.

ERUPTION When a volcano throws lava, gas, and ash onto the Earth's surface.

FACE A flat side of a crystal. Some crystals have many, many faces, and others only have a few faces, depending on the crystal shape.

FIBROUS A mineral that looks like it's made of fibers or cloth.

FINE Mineral grains that are so tiny you can't easily see them.

FLUORESCENT MINERALS Minerals that glow under a special ultraviolet light.

GEM A mineral specimen that is valuable, often brightly colored and transparent.

GEODE A round rock that is hollow inside, often with a lining of crystals.

GLASSY A mineral that is very shiny, just like glass.

GRANITIC If a type of rock is related to granite, or resembles granite, we call it "granitic."

GRAIN The little particles of minerals inside rocks. Some can be very big, or coarse, and others can be tiny, or fine.

IGNEOUS ROCK Rocks that form when molten rock cools off and hardens; this can happen deep inside the Earth or on the Earth's surface.

LAVA Melted rocks that have been pushed onto the Earth's surface.

LUSTER How shiny a mineral is.

MAGMA Melted rocks that are still deep underground.

METAL Shiny, bendable minerals that form naturally, like copper.

METAMORPHIC ROCK Rocks that form when older rocks are heated up and pressed on by lots of weight; this changes the old rocks into new types.

MINERAL A substance that forms when a pure chemical hardens. Minerals form as crystals inside rocks.

MOLTEN Melted and able to flow, like liquid.

OPAQUE Not see-through; letting no light into it.

ROCK A group of minerals that formed together in a tight mass. Rocks can form inside the Earth or on the Earth's surface. There are three kinds of rock: igneous, sedimentary, and metamorphic, and they all formed in a different way.

SAND Tiny particles of rocks and minerals that have been worn down by weathering.

SEDIMENT Little particles of rocks, minerals, and even plants and animals that have been worn down by weathering. Sediments are things like sand, dust, and mud.

SEDIMENTARY ROCK Rocks that form when sediment sticks together and hardens. This mostly happens in or near water, especially lakes and oceans.

SPECIMEN A collectible piece of a rock or mineral.

TECTONIC PLATE The large sheets of rock that make up the Earth's crust. They move around and bump into each other, which causes earthquakes and volcanoes.

TRANSLUCENT Something that lets a little light through, but you still can't see through it.

TRANSPARENT Something that lets lots of light through; it is clear and see-through.

VEIN A stripe of mineral that formed inside a crack in a rock.

VOLCANO An opening, or vent, in the ground where molten rock and gas is forced upwards onto the Earth's surface.

WAXY A mineral that is a little shiny and reflects light the same way wax does.

WEATHERING When water, wind, ice, and plants break and wear down rocks and minerals.

RECOMMENDED READING FOR KIDS

Tomecek, Steve. *National Geographic Kids: Everything Rocks and Minerals*. National Geographic, 2011.

Dorling Kindersley (DK). *The Rock and Gem Book: And other Treasures of the Natural World,* 2016.

RECOMMENDED READING FOR OLDER READERS

Bates, Robert L., editor. *Dictionary of Geological Terms*, 3rd Edition. New York: Anchor Books, 1984.

Bonewitz, Ronald Louis. *Smithsonian Rock and Gem.* New York: DK Publishing, 2005.

Chesteman, Charles W. *The Audubon Society Field Guide to North American Rocks and Minerals.* New York: Knopf, 1979.

Johnsen, Ole. *Minerals of the World.* New Jersey: Princeton University Press, 2004.

Mottana, Annibale, et al. *Simon and Schuster's Guide to Rocks and Minerals.* New York: Simon and Schuster, 1978.

Pellant, Chris. *Rocks and Minerals.* New York: Dorling Kindersley Publishing, 2002.

Pough, Frederick H. *Rocks and Minerals.* Boston: Houghton Mifflin, 1988.

Robinson, George W. *Minerals*. New York: Simon & Schuster, 1994.

Rocks and Mineral Journal
KEEP TRACK OF YOUR FINDS

Date: _____

Where I Found It: _____

_____

_____

Is It a Rock or a Mineral?: _____

What I Think It Is: _____

Date: _____

Where I Found It: _____

_____

_____

Is It a Rock or a Mineral?: _____

What I Think It Is: _____

KEEP TRACK OF YOUR FINDS

Date: _____

Where I Found It: _____

_____

_____

Is It a Rock or a Mineral?: _____

What I Think It Is: _____

Date: _____

Where I Found It: _____

_____

_____

Is It a Rock or a Mineral?: _____

What I Think It Is: _____

KEEP TRACK OF YOUR FINDS

Date: _____

Where I Found It: _____

_____

_____

Is It a Rock or a Mineral?: _____

What I Think It Is: _____

Date: _____

Where I Found It: _____

_____

_____

Is It a Rock or a Mineral?: _____

What I Think It Is: _____

KEEP TRACK OF YOUR FINDS

Date:

Where I Found It:

Is It a Rock or a Mineral?:

What I Think It Is:

Date:

Where I Found It:

Is It a Rock or a Mineral?:

What I Think It Is:

KEEP TRACK OF YOUR FINDS

Date: _____

Where I Found It: _____

_____

_____

Is It a Rock or a Mineral?: _____

What I Think It Is: _____

Date: _____

Where I Found It: _____

_____

_____

Is It a Rock or a Mineral?: _____

What I Think It Is: _____

KEEP TRACK OF YOUR FINDS

Date: _____

Where I Found It: _____

_____

_____

Is It a Rock or a Mineral?: _____

What I Think It Is: _____

Date: _____

Where I Found It: _____

_____

_____

Is It a Rock or a Mineral?: _____

What I Think It Is: _____

ABOUT THE AUTHOR

Dan R. Lynch grew up in a rock shop, learning to identify rocks and minerals from a very young age. He has written a number of books on rock and mineral identification, with a special focus on agates from his home region of northern Minnesota and Lake Superior. He has always loved the natural world, especially all of its wonderful little details that many people don't pay any attention to, and he hopes that this book can spark young readers' curiosity about the rocks beneath their feet. Dan currently lives in Madison, Wisconsin, with his lovely wife, Julie Kirsch, and Daisy, their fluffy white cat.